The Inspirational Leader

Inspire Your team to Believe In The Impossible

GIFFORD THOMAS

PRIASE FOR THE INSPIRATIONAL LEADER

Perfect read for both new and experienced leaders!

"Even the most experienced leaders need a source of inspiration from time to time! The Inspirational Leader: Inspire Your Team to Believe The Impossible offers some great insights into the best approaches to leadership. Was well written and a very easy read....." **Alison Browne**

Love your Book

"I'm young in the field of Human Resources management. I have 5 years experience and I want to grow more I love your book everyday I put up something on my WhatsApp status from the reading. Would love to be under your wings to grow and become a good servant of Human Resources. Keep up the good work!" **Marsha Barrow Smith**

Great Book

"Great book Gifford, I wanted to share this review of it. Any reader will benefit from it." **Mike Temple**

An Excellent Read

An excellent read, very well written, great content that crosses all organizational line, horizontally & vertically! **Richard Dye**

Love the book

Love the book....what I have read so far is a work of art! Thank you for sharing your insights! **Neal Golub**

DEDICATION

This book is dedicated to all the people who have desire to become great leaders, who have a desire to think differently, who have a desire to be inspirational, and who have a desire to believe in the impossible. This book is dedicated to you.

CONTENTS

ACKNOWLEDGMENTS

Special thanks to my beautiful wife and 3 children for all their support and to my 600,000+ Leadership First family.

INTRODUCTION

Dr. Martin Luther King, Jr.

O n the 28th of August 1963, Dr. Martin Luther King Jr. inspired people around the world with a message of peaceful resistance and racial equality. His famous speech, "I HAVE A DREAM," which he gave in front of the Lincoln Memorial, on the 28th of August 1963, to a crowd of over 200,000 people, helped to inspire the world to think differently about race. He inspired people by his non-violence approach to his protest, and he inspired people to dream of a world where "little white boys and little white girls, will be able to hold hands with little black boys and black girls, as sisters and brothers."

Nelson Mandela

Nelson Mandela was a great pioneer who helped bring an end to apartheid in South Africa. Although he was imprisoned for 27 years due to his anti-apartheid actions, he was released and later became his country's first black president in 1994. Mandela inspired the world with his advocacy for peace, racial unity, social justice, and forgiveness. He was a champion of the people, and spent 95 years building his legacy until his death in 2013.

Rosa Parks

T ired from a full day's work, Rosa Parks boarded a Montgomery bus on December 1, 1955, and forever became one of the people who changed the world. She was arrested for civil disobedience when she refused to obey the driver's order to give up her seat and move to the back of the bus so a white person could sit there. Parks' act of defiance inspired the Montgomery Bus Boycott, which was considered a pivotal moment in the civil rights movement.

Muhammad Ali

Muhammad Ali became a champion of the civil rights and African American interests, his refusal to fight in the Vietnam War cost him his boxing license. Still his principle stance inspired the world to believe in something more than their own self-preservation.

Mother Teresa

Mother Teresa sought to identify w the unloved and destitute. She poverty and service to the pc people to become of service to people in need,

W

speak with

in his pur

timid youn

fear, to be

principle f

people to b

Mahatma Gandhi

*T*Who would have imagined that the shy and introverted boy who refused to stay back after school to interact with his classmates for fear of being laughed at, would be able to such eloquence and persuasion, winning over the whole nation uit for India's independence? Who would have expected the lawyer, who scrammed the courtrooms at the slightest tinge of ble to stand up against tyranny and injustice, to become later the gurehead of the Indian's independence movement, inspiring lieve that the impossible is possible?

Oprah Winfrey

In 1983, Oprah Winfrey relocated to Chicago to host WLS-TV's low-rated half-hour morning talk-show, AM Chicago. The first episode aired on January 2, 1984. Within months after Winfrey took over, the show went from the last place in the ratings to overtaking all talk-shows as the highest-rated talk show in Chicago. It was renamed The Oprah Winfrey Show, expanded to a full hour, and broadcast nationally beginning September 8, 1986. After 25 years, the show ended in 2011 and Winfrey is arguably the world's most powerful woman that inspired the world to believe that you can become anything you want, if you only believe in yourself.

Jeff Bezos

Amazon is undeniably a retail behemoth with over 150 million unique monthly visitors. But while most view Bezos as an empire-builder, the roots of his success run deep. When Amazon first launched in 1995 as a website that only sold books according to Avery Hartmans, founder Jeff Bezos had a vision for the company's explosive growth and e-commerce domination. After leaving his job as a vice president at D.E. Shaw & Co, a Wall Street-based investment banking firm, many felt Bezos made the biggest mistake of his life. However, Bezos found the inspiration within to ignore the naysayers and follow his heart to start Amazon, which turned out to be the most valuable company in the world.

Can you point to the common themes among all these great leaders:

- They followed the feeling in their heart

- They were visionary

- They never gave up despite their challenging situations

- They never lost sight of their purpose

- They all stayed true to their core values

- They did not allow people's opinion of them to become a distraction

- They believed in the impossible

- They are all very inspirational leaders

Inspiration and leadership are inseparable; if you cannot inspire your team to achieve greatness, if you cannot inspire a group of people to follow your vision by your words and actions, you're not a leader. You're an average manager at best. Inspirational leaders don't accept "the way life is," and they are often uncomfortable if they do not live their purpose and share it with the world. We were all born with unique gifts to share, but we are often thrown off track by taking a job that is safe, and has great benefits but isn't fulfilling.

We may be good at it, we may be the best at it, but it does not bring out the greatness trap inside of us begging to come out. The Inspirational Leader, Inspire Your Team to Believe in The Impossible, was written to help all leaders successfully navigate all the disruptions in today's fiercely competitive world. We need a new generation of leaders who care deeply for the well-being of their team and understand that their people are the heart of their leadership.

Whether you are the leaders of a large, medium, or small organization, a Teacher, a Father, a Mother, CEO, VP, Team Lead, Manager, Police Officer, or a Hustler. This book was written to help you inspire your team to believe in the impossible. To become a great and inspirational leader, you cannot allow your life to be ruled by people and events; you must own your leadership by empowering and pushing yourself to follow that dream and feeling in your heart. It is interesting, Harvard Business School gathered data from assessments of more than 50,000 leaders, and the ability to inspire stood out as one of the most critical competencies.

Inspiration creates the highest levels of engagement, it is what separates the best leaders from everyone else, and it is what employees want most in their leaders. Bain & company's research, identified 33 distinct and tangible attributes that are statistically significant in creating inspiration in others, according to Mark Horwitch and Meredith Whipple Callahan. The power of a company with leaders who inspire at every level up and down the organization is hard to overstate. These companies consistently pull off innovative or heroic feats in business because so many of the people who work there are motivated and inspired to make them happen.

Leadership is about people. It's about inspiring people to believe that the impossible is possible; it's about developing and building people to perform at heights they never imagine. It's about self-discovery and becoming a slave for your gift. It's about making a positive impact on your community, your company, your department, your employees, and the world. Each chapter in this book will push you to become the leader you were destined to be; a leader of influence, a leader of value, a leader of vision, and most importantly, an inspirational leader who can inspire your team to believe in the impossible.

1. THE LEADERSHIP CHALLENGE - WHY 70% OF MANAGERS FAIL TO BECOME INSPIRATIONAL LEADERS

foundr foundr   ...

Warren Buffett
@itswarenbuffett

Surround yourself with people that push you to do better. No drama or negativity. Just higher goals and higher motivation. Good times and positive energy. No jealousy or hate. Simply bringing out the absolute best in each other.

A couple of months ago, I read a post on LinkedIn from Chelene Pedro about a CEO, who was very nasty and disrespectful to one of his managers. The guy shouted so loudly, everyone down the corridor knew he didn't like the size of the font. The manager walked out of the CEO's office and returned with a handwritten resignation letter dated, "effective immediately." Can you blame him! How in God's green earth do you expect anyone to function in that type of environment, and I am 100% sure this manager is not the first employee to face that type of abuse from that CEO.

This story really stuck with me, and I can understand why 70% of managers fail to become leaders, they fondly call themselves leaders, but their actions and behavior say something totally different. Harvard Business School scholar John Kotter has argued that there are three fundamentals processes for effective leadership that many managers have failed to grasp.

- **Establishing a compelling direction, a vision for the future, and the strategies for how to get there.**

- **Aligning people, communicating the direction, building shared understanding, getting people to believe in the vision, and persuading and influencing people to follow that vision.**

- **Motivating and inspiring people to enact the kind of change that you have articulated.**

Kotter further argued that finding people with leadership potential is much more complicated than finding people who are good managers. Since driving change is much more difficult than striving for efficiency and meeting near-term financial and non-financial targets. The renowned leadership expert Warren Bennis, who authored 30 leadership books, including one of my favourite, On Becoming a Leader, indicated that "a leader is not simply someone who experiences the personal exhilaration of being in charge." A leader is someone whose actions have the most profound consequences on other people's lives, for better or for worse, sometimes forever and ever."

When you are responsible for managing and leading people, you have an opportunity to make a profound impact on your team, but it's up to you as the leader to recognize that your team is the organisation's most valuable resource. As the leader, your influence can change the trajectory of someone's life, professionally as well as personally. During one of Simon Sinek's trips with the Marines Corps, he recalls a particularly harrowing situation in Afghanistan.

A pilot provided cover for troops under fire, exposing himself to life-threatening enemy fire from both sides of a valley in Afghanistan. According to Sinek, there was so much enemy fire that the tracer fire—the streaks of light that follow the bullets—lit up the whole area. Shells and rockets all aimed at the middle, all aimed squarely at the Special Operations Forces pinned down below.

The pilot, without hesitation, together with his wing-man, provided the cover needed for the Special Forces to come out of that battle with no casualties. Trapped in a dangerous spot, the pilot shows the true meaning of leadership and service. He acted bravely, giving to others without expectation of anything in return. When asked the question, why would anyone do such a thing? The pilot answered, "because they would've done it for me.

This is what it means to work in a place in which the leaders create a circle of safety for their team and, in return, their people giving everything they've got to protect and advance the well-being of one another, their leader and their organization. There's no excuse for any 'so-called leader' to abuse their employees. None!

I have seen with my own two eyes, CEOs and managers taking pleasure in this kind of nasty behavior. Because they know, and in many instances have convinced their employees that their company is the only one to work for, no other option exists. I can remember attending a departmental meeting scheduled by the CEO. This guy was trying his best to brainwash the staff to believe that if anyone leaves the company, they will be unemployed for four years. The CEO was so brazen; he even asked people to raise their hands if they believe they will get a job within the four years; only four employees, myself included, out of the 35 or so employees raise their hands.

You have to be very careful about the people who call themselves a leader, especially the ones with Pseudo - Leadership tendencies, we will address this in chapter 6, and you will understand why many of these so-called leaders are only concerned about their own well-being, nothing else. When people are void of inspiration, they must seek ways to keep themselves moving toward a clearly defined end state. According to Frederika Roberts, I believe that true leaders are inspirational. They exert a positive influence over their colleagues, and they are essential to business success.

As Greg Savage points out in his article, "People don't leave Companies, they leave Leaders,' when employees leave it's not "the company" they blame. It's not the location, or the team, or the database, or the air-conditioning. It's the leadership! When people are valued, it's incredible how their whole aura shines brightly. They feel a sense of importance, and it gives them the inspiration to produce their very best work.

How do you value your people?

When Pepsico CEO Indra Nooyi traveled to India to visit her mother for the first time after being named CEO, something happens on that visit that change Indra Nooyi perspective on leadership. At her mother's house, a steady stream of family and friends came into the house. They'd went right over to her mother and said, "Congratulations." Or "You did such a good job raising Indra."

According to Indra Nooyi, "Watching them, I realized I'd never done for our senior executives at PepsiCo what my mother's family and friends were doing for her. So, as soon as I got back, I decided to send a letter thanking the parents of some of our executives. And since then, I've sent similar letters to spouses.

These letters' impact has led to some of the most meaningful experiences I've had at PepsiCo. If I have one request for those of you reading this who lead people, try this. The reactions you get will move you more than you can know."

As the leader of your department or company, have you ever

- Send a birthday card to your employee's children
- Asked your employees how they are going
- Asked your employees how's their mom or dad going
- Or taking Indra Nooyi advice and sending a thank you card to your employee's mother or father

If you never did, try it; these simple things will make a massive difference with your employee's motivation and inspiration. When you show your employees the simplest of gratitude and genuinely, and I stress on the word GENUINELY, make your employee's family part of the company, you will have some of the most loyal employees.

As a leader, you have an incredible opportunity to change someone's life every single day. It could be something as simple as saying hello, writing a handwritten note stating you did an excellent job today or remembering your employee's names when greeting them. Some leaders take these things for granted, but believe me; your employees will feel valued. Leadership is all about people, the little things make a huge difference, and the organizations that get it are the ones that ultimately succeed.

Leadership is never about tearing people down and making people feel less than themselves. Leadership is about people; it's about inspiring people to believe that the impossible is possible. It's about developing and building people to perform at heights they never imagine. It's about making a positive impact on your community, your company, your department, your employees, and by extension, the world. According to Charlene, if you want to be a great leader, you must first start with being a better human being.

2. LEADERSHIP REQUIRES THAT YOU BUILD A RELATIONSHIP WITH YOUR TEAM, HERE'S WHY.

> OUTSTANDING LEADERS GO OUT OF THEIR WAY TO BOOST THE SELF-ESTEEM OF THEIR PERSONNEL. IF PEOPLE BELIEVE IN THEMSELVES, IT'S AMAZING WHAT THEY CAN ACCOMPLISH.

A newly minted sales manager held a meeting with her staff to discuss the company's shortfall for the past quarter. One of her sales agents missed her targets, and the manager became verbally abusive to the agent in front of the entire team. But what happened next shocked the whole team.

Within a week of the incident, the sales agent resigns. The manager found out later that the agent was in a bitter divorce and custody battle with her ex-husband that took a toll on her life personally, emotionally, and professionally. Now some people will read this and think well you need to leave your personal issues at home because work is work right! If you have personal issues, deal with it; the company is not responsible for helping you. I heard this from someone I had a conversation with, and it is always amazing when I encounter "leaders" who treat their people like commodities as opposed to people, you know a human being with a heart and feeling. But what is even more bizarre is that these "leaders" would complain that their company is not living up to its potential.

Leadership requires that you build a relationship with your team. If one of your people is dealing with a significant personal issue and you are oblivious to it, or your employee chooses not to talk to you or even mention it, then something is wrong with the culture, or worse, the company is over-manage and under-led.

I read this story once about someone who experienced an extraordinary moment at their job during a very challenging project with his team. The CEO of the company, sensing something was wrong, gave a compelling and motivational speech that left each person believing that they can achieve anything.

Half an hour later, everyone left the room looking at each other and saying: "Yes, let's do; let's go for it." Usually, managers can drive businesses, but what separates the great companies from the good ones is inspirational leaders. According to Fernando Vilas, these leaders can inspire others to follow them, even in very adverse situations.

For example, inspirational leaders can transmit a message to each person in their team. They spread enthusiasm and integrity, acting as a role model. They are great at setting real-life examples that make people identify with them. These leaders can leverage the meaning of goals and tasks. Their emotions are magnetic, touching the most buried feeling inside of their people. They give purpose to the organization, explaining the personal reasons to achieve them as opposed to following an order from a manager. Contrary to what managers usually do, they develop each employee individually, with full credibility.

They understand their employees' needs, and they genuinely care about them. They give their people the importance they deserve by soliciting feedback and engaging their people in personal topics as well. They enter into real valuable dialogues that build a healthy relationship between leader and follower.

That's what leaders do, that's what leadership is all about. If you have no relationship with your team and you are comfortable with your people coming to work, completing their task, and leaving with no type of interaction, please, do us a favor and don't call yourself a leader.

By the way, can you guess the sales manager's reaction when she found out about the agent situation? Yes, you guess right, the manager showed no remorse and indicated that any agent's personal problem is not her problem; her only concern is meeting and exceeding her targets.

What a company to work for!

3. LOVE THE PEOPLE YOU LEAD

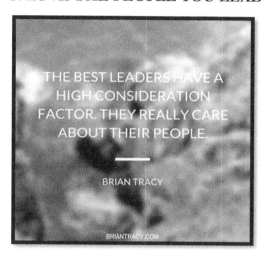

THE BEST LEADERS HAVE A HIGH CONSIDERATION FACTOR. THEY REALLY CARE ABOUT THEIR PEOPLE.

BRIAN TRACY

BRIANTRACY.COM

In 2008 when Howard Schultz came back as CEO of Starbucks, he used a word that made many of his business associates uncomfortable. Love! Howard said his love for Starbucks gave him the inspiration to come back as CEO and to help the company become the leader in their industry again.

Legendary hall of fame football coach Vince Lombardi, who is arguably one of the greatest coaches in the history of the NFL, said: "I don't necessarily have to like my players and associates, but as their leader, I must love them. Love is loyalty; love is teamwork; love respects the dignity of the individual. This is the strength of any organization. **If you want to be a leader today, it's not about whether you like people. If you're going to be a leader today, you have to LOVE people, period.**

Love is at the heart of leadership, especially servant leadership, and if we're to thrive in our organizations and communities, we need a great deal more of it in our leadership today. According to Simon Sinek, "The leader who gets the most out of their people, are the leaders who care most about their people."

In all my years of experience, working in many organizations, I have never heard any of my former managers and note the word managers, mention the word love, not once. Why is love such a taboo word in many organizations? According to Adam Meyer, an executive director of UCF's Student Accessibility Services, we use the word "love" to reference many things in our daily lives and culture. We love family, friends, pizza, ice cream, our favorite sports teams, and more.

So why can't we love the people we work with. Love the people we lead, love the work our people are doing, and communicate that love through our actions and words. Lombardi was viewed as a hard-driving, tough football coach, for example, but one who loved his players dearly, and was passionate about growing members of his team in a highly intimate and personal way. In Kevin Cashman's article, The Three L's of Leadership: Love, Listen, and Leap, Kevin had the opportunity to coach many of Lombardi's former players who transitioned into their business career, all of whom spoke about Lombardi in an entirely different light.

Many of his players said, "I have never been so loved by someone outside my family. We all knew he would do anything for us...anything. We would go through walls for this man." Lombardi earned the right to drive his talent to the limit because his intense drive, was balanced by his equally fierce caring. According to Lolly Daskal, the most critical factor that differentiates a good leader from a great leader is LOVE. Yes, love! The best leaders want to be liked; they want openness from others; they want to be understood, appreciated, and communicated with. Leaders who do not care and are cold-hearted or cold-blooded are not very successful. When you **Lead With Love**, success follows, and one of the best chemistry a leader can have with their team is their **genuine care** and deep appreciation for every member of that team.

Managers can drive businesses, but what separates the great companies from the good ones is leaders who care. According to Fernando Vilas, these leaders inspire others to follow them, even in very adverse situations. They are capable of transmitting a message to each person in their team, touching the most buried feeling inside of their people.

They give purpose to the organization, explaining the personal reasons to achieve them instead of following an order from a manager. They understand their employees' needs, and they **genuinely care** about them. Not care about them when they want something done or when it suits their interest or purpose, but genuinely caring irrespective of the situation. They give their team the importance they deserve by soliciting feedback and engaging their people in topics of a personal nature. They enter into real valuable dialogues that build a healthy relationship between the leader and their team.

A simple thing like asking how are you going, how's your son or your daughter, how's your mother or your father going. These simple things add tons of value to your leadership and develop a healthy bond between the leader and his/her team. One of the best places to begin in leading with love is to exhibit much patience and kindness toward other people (without forgoing accountability and expectations), to always hope for and to see the best in others even in the most challenging of situations, and to seek the highest good in all that is done.

According to Adam Meyer, this is easier said than done; it is scary to think about intentionally putting your wants and needs behind others' wants and needs. However, loving others and living for others is tremendously more rewarding; since you cannot call yourself an inspirational leader if you do not **genuinely care** about every member of your team. You cannot lead effectively if you do not love the people you are leading.

In Dede Henley's article, Three Ways Great Leaders Show They Care About Their Team; Henley shared a story about a large healthcare company with 74,000 employees, that conducted a management development program for five days for all their clinic managers. The CEO of the company holds a "town hall meeting," where he fields questions and shares whatever information is helpful. More importantly, he communicates, personally and individually, that he cares about every one of those 24 clinic managers.

How does he manage to connect in a meaningful manner with each of those managers? He asks his assistant to compile a document with each clinic manager's photo, name, and important information about them — a son or daughter graduating, a recent surgery, a big win at work. Before he steps into the room, he memorizes this information. Once there, he's able to address every person by name and ask them about their lives. It takes time and attention to do this, but the impact is worth it. People felt **genuinely cared** about. Now, is this CEO focused on results? Sure is. Is he focused on company growth? Ultimately, yes. But at that moment, his focus is on a different job entirely. His attention is focused on communicating with his team that he cares. And that's your job as a leader too. To become an inspirational leader and to get the very best from your team, you must love your people and show that you **genuinely care** about them professionally as well as personally.

4. LEADING WITHOUT FEAR, INTIMIDATION OR AUTHORITY

Molly's employees are fiercely loyal to her, everyone respects her, and they are highly successful as individuals and a team. By contrast, other leaders in the organization report that their people seem disengaged, they experience high staff turnover, and their results are often disappointing. So, what does Molly do that other leaders don't? To begin with, Molly regularly reminds her team members of the purpose of their work. She knows that she is a role model for her team, demonstrating integrity in all of her working relationships.

She sets high expectations, but "walks the walk" to demonstrate the standards that she expects. Molly enjoys the perks of being an inspirational leader, which allows her team to help their organization achieve its objectives and fulfil its purpose. **Effective leadership is the most critical**

factor for organizational success in the 21st century, and the old pyramid structure won't suffice, according to Sheri Nasim, president and CEO of the San Diego-based Center for Executive Excellence. She said "companies that want to continue to grow need to embrace transformational leadership" during her presentation at the recent The Future of Work conference.

Millennials are changing the world of work, and if you don't accept the fact that our work will be completely different in the next 10 - 15 years, your organization will get left behind. The pyramid structure of the 20th century, according to Erin Binney, worked when manufacturing companies employed most of the workers, and the employment contract was strictly transactional. In this system, employees came to work, did their jobs, collected wages, and went home.

Leading by fear and intimidation was the order of the day. There was a physical and emotional distance between leaders and employees. Leaders sat in offices removed from the manufacturing floor and viewed employees only as a cost of labor, not as individuals with lives outside of work. Unfortunately, many companies are operating with this ideology where communication is stagnated, and silos are the order of the day. Leaders have a vested interest in building bureaucracy and protecting the status quo to keep their jobs, even though this isn't necessarily in the company's best interests.

Many organizations have changed and modified their culture and changed the style of their leadership because they recognized that this generation is completely different from the baby boomers who believed in a job for life. Many leaders now are very inspirational, and many organizations are now purpose and values-driven, more involved in societal issues, and moved away from the annual performance reviews. They developed and implemented policies that strive to provide a work-life balance, flexible work hours, and a host of other things that genuinely seek the interest and development of their employees.

Leaders of the future must change their leadership style to give their organization any chance to compete and operate in this technologically driven world. The speed of change is unprecedented in the history of our existence on this planet. Leaders must modify their leadership to attract the best talent available to ensure their people are inspired every day to go the extra mile.

How do you get your team to go the extra mile, consider the following;

- Communicate with every member of your team. Inspirational leaders are capable of transmitting a message to each person on their team. These leaders are capable of leveraging the meaning of goals and tasks. Their emotions are magnetic, touching the most buried feeling inside of their people.

- They question old ways of doing things, impart new perspectives, and, most importantly, challenge the status quo.

- They develop each employee individually, with full credibility. They understand their employees' needs, and they genuinely care about them.

Building Great Teams

It takes great leadership to build great teams, and winning teams are developed under leaders who can flex and bend their own personalities around each team member's needs. According to Glenn Llopis, team building is both an art and a science, and the leader who can consistently build high-performance teams is worth their weight in gold. When you manage each team member individually, you maximize their strengths and learn how to fill in for their weaker areas. This is what true support is all about. Supported teams are successful teams. Leaders are only as successful as their teams, and the great ones know that with the right team dynamics, decisions, and diverse personalities, everyone wins.

A "team" is not just people who work at the same time in the same place. A real team is a group of very different individuals who enjoy working together and who share a commitment to working cohesively to help the organization achieve their common goals and to fulfil its purpose. Most likely, they are not all equal in experience, talent, or education, but they are similar in one vitally important way, their commitment to the good of the organization. A leader's role is greatly diminished without their team, and any group of people your family, your workplace, or your community will get the best results by working as a team.

One of the most distinctive traits of great leaders is their ability to inspire, motivate, challenge, and support their people to succeed and grow. When a leader can inspire and empower their employees to become the very best version of themselves, by challenging their assumptions of what they can accomplish, a leader can now empower their team to believe in the impossible. When you trust your team and give them more responsibility, it can benefit both the people and the business and, at the same time, create a great workplace culture that allows everyone to contribute towards the attainment of the organization's purpose.

Many leaders seem to forget that leading others more than anything else should be held in reverence. Being the leader means that you have been placed in a position to serve others. Too many times, I have seen leaders duck and cover, throw their team under the bus, throw their positional weight around, and instead of leading from a place of service, lead from a place of ego when things get rough.

You are privileged to be in a position where you can direct, shape, and focus people's potential to a specific result. When you are given the responsibility to lead, you are given an awesome opportunity to influence the lives of many people positively; a responsibility you should never take for granted.

"No one can be a great leader unless they care about everyone on their team."

An organization's culture doesn't turn toxic because of a few bad seeds. It becomes toxic because the leadership didn't see or outright ignored the signs that something was amiss. Leadership sets the tone of the workplace culture and acceptable behavior patterns, according to Shahnaz Broucek, a professor of coaching and mentoring for MBA students at the University of Michigan. Nobody ever said that being a leader is easy. It's very simple to bark out orders and dismiss someone if they are not performing, but it takes work to coach, mentor, inspires, and motivate your team to perform at their optimum best. That's the fundamental difference between a leader and manager; You must be willing to pay the price of leadership if you want the perks of leadership, according to John Maxwell.

As a leader, create a culture where your people are inspired to create great ideas, where the dreamers are encouraged to dream big dreams and to lift the organization to a higher level of performance continually. Ultimately, the onus is on the leadership to promote a high trust culture; to identify and fix the source of a team's disintegration. But what if leadership is the problem? Hmm, great question, this means the leader must get it right with themselves first before they can get it right with their team.

Molly's leadership provided a great example of what great leadership can accomplish without fear, intimidation, or authority. When you understand that leadership is about people, inspiring people to believe that the impossible is possible. Developing and building people to perform at heights they never imagine while making a positive impact on your community, your company, your department, your employees, and the world. When you recognized that leadership is all about people, your company will be among the best in the world.

5. BUILDING A SERVANT LEADERSHIP CULTURE USING THESE 4 SIMPLE STEPS

> TRUE LEADERSHIP IS SERVANT HOOD. PUT THE INTEREST OF OTHERS AT THE CENTER OF YOUR DECISIONS.
>
> Dave Ramsey

Gandhi once stated, "the best way to find yourself is to lose yourself in the service of others."

NO truer words have been spoken, and nothing encapsulates the spirit of servant leadership more than these great words from Mahatma Gandhi. Exemplary leaders like Mother Theresa, Nelson Mandela, Dr. Martin Luther King Jr., according to Eric Lau, have all shown the impactful nature of servant leadership. Some have argued, how can one be a leader and a servant at the same time? Is it possible?

The answer is a resounding **YES!** In 2008, at the height of the global financial crisis, a St. Louis based company Barry-Wehmiller, lost 30% of its orders due to the effects of the recession. The CEO, Bob Chapman, got together with the board of directors to discuss layoffs, and what's the very first strategy many companies used to save money; job cuts. But Bob Chapman refused to let any of his employees go because every member of his team of over 2000 plus employees, was considered family. In the end, the board devised a furlough program, through which every employee would be required to take four weeks of unpaid vacation. The creation of the program at least meant that everyone was safe, morale went up, and the company saved $20 million.

Bob is the type of CEO who always puts his people before his numbers, and feels a sense of responsibility in making sure everyone who works at his organization, feels fulfilled and engaged in the work they do. How many CEO's out there do you know can say that? When you are called to lead, you are invited to serve. You become the servant because leadership is all about being of service to others. A leader with a servant's heart is a truly invaluable asset; they work tirelessly to develop their people and focus on what they can do for others. How can you develop a heart for servant leadership, and how can you establish a culture of servant leadership at your company, follow these four simple steps.

Change your mindset

Robert Greenleaf, the founder of the modern servant leadership movement, describes a servant leadership mindset as one that begins with the desire to serve by meeting others' needs. To embrace the spirit of servant leadership, you must first change your mindset and focus on providing service to others. Great leaders are always seeking to improve and enhance something or someone. This is very important; to become one of the greats of leadership, you must first develop a habit of service.

Lead by example

Most leaders know that their actions can influence how a team feels and performs. However, when leaders don't practice what they preach, you can almost see the staff's loss of enthusiasm and goodwill. Once a leader's character is proven untrustworthy, their ability to lead will diminish. If you want a culture of servant leadership at your organization, as the leader, you must walk the talk and lead by example.

Make the environment safe.

You have to give your team a safe place to share their ideas and opinions without malice, judgment, victimization, or condemnation. A servant leader must be able to listen to others and to be very receptive to what is being said. They may not always agree, but they are very responsive to someone's position without undermining them.

Build a culture of leadership throughout the entire company

A company with a leadership culture expects all employees, not just those with "VP" or "Chief" in their titles, but all their people, to think and act like leaders. What separates the good leaders from the great leaders is their ability to build a culture of leadership throughout their organization that cultivates great leaders.

Bringing all together, embracing a servant leader mindset at all levels of an organization, can transform any organization's culture. A leader with a heart for servant leadership must lead by example, and inspire his/her team to lose themselves in service to others. This will help their team achieve their higher calling, and propel the company to become one of the best in the world.

6. FOCUS ON YOUR LEADERSHIP CHARACTER

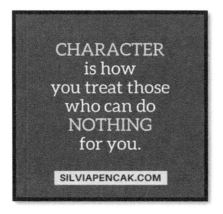

Two years ago, somewhere around October, I was dealing with a crisis that challenged my sanity. I have always been cool and calm under pressure circumstances, but this one, wow! Tested my mental. One morning, while I was driving my daughter to school, my facial expression changed, and quite honestly, I wasn't even aware, my daughter said "daddy why are you looking so angry," with a pitiful worried look on her face.

Her eyes began to swell with tears because she never saw her daddy looked like that before. At that moment, I immediately check myself and I said Gifford, you need to take control of yourself, you cannot allow one challenge to derail you like that. I learned a lesson from that situation, **how you react to crisis shows your real character as a leader.** Nothing reveals the actual state of your character better than how you handled your last crisis. There's much more to leadership than having a title and being in charge of a team.

You might have the authority to tell people what to do, but if you're an ineffective leader and your character is questionable, you won't be able to guide, influence, inspire and motivate anyone to accomplish anything. As an inspirational leader, you cannot have an unpredictable leadership character, which changes with every passing wind. One criticism of Steve Job's leadership before he was ousted from Apple, was his immature leadership and how unpredictable he was every day. His character was very questionable, and people were not sure which Steve Jobs will show up to the office daily.

No one should think he/she is too smart or too safe to avoid the consequences of a lack of character. Former Wall Street mogul Bernie Madoff operated "the biggest Ponzi scheme in history he bilked his clients of billions of dollars and fooled regulators for decades. Madoff was convicted of securities fraud, investment advisor fraud, wire and mail fraud, money laundering, filing false documents with the Securities and Exchange Commission, making false statements, perjury, and taking from employee's benefit funds. He was sentenced to 150 years in prison.

Your real leadership character will show up sooner or later, and people will eventually know if you are a fraud, or if you are a genuine leader. For example, Theresa Gattung is the CEO of Telecom NZ, a New Zealand telecommunications company. Her candor about her vulnerabilities, as well as her philosophy on leadership, has won her the admiration of her male colleagues. She recognizes that good leadership consists more of character than personality: When Sheryl Sandberg's husband died unexpectedly, Sandberg said it felt like a void, like it was sucking me in and pushing on me, pulling me in, and I couldn't even see or breathe. Sandberg was honest with her feeling, and she made it known to the world. The process provided the most critical leadership lesson of all time; there is nothing wrong with being vulnerable as a leader because it shows your true leadership character.

Be honest about your feelings.

According to Shawn Doyle, many people think that revealing your feelings as a leader is a sign of weakness, but nothing can be further from the truth. When Howard Schultz returned as Starbucks CEO in 2007 during the worst decline in the company history, with tears in his eyes, Schultz emotionally said to all employees, if the company does not change, Starbucks as a company will be no more.

"There are moments where you've got to share your soul and your conscience with people and show them who you are and not be afraid of it" Howard Schultz

Schultz indicated the need to be open and honest, but even more, he allowed himself to be vulnerable to connect with his employees. As a result, Starbucks experienced a spectacular recovery and cemented its status as one of the world's best brands. Vulnerability is hardly a trait many leaders race to embrace, according to Sheryl, but it can build deeper relationships and loyalty, enabling people to bring their whole selves to work. You should be working in an environment where you can bring your whole self to work.

If you look at a statue, any statue does it change in the day; in the night; in the snow; in the rain; in a hurricane; an earthquake; does it move; does it get upset or lose it cool; that's what we called character. When people can predict what you will do in your absence, you have developed a leadership character people can trust. That's why leaders with character achieve results that transcend everyday organizational imperatives. Authentic leadership always begins with the inner person, according to John Maxwell.

The character of a leader will filter into the entire organization, influencing everyone who works there. Great character will create the potential for a great organization. But, it all begins with the leader's heart. Authentic and inspirational leaders, by acting on a core set of benevolent values brings out the best in their followers, and do great things for society. The question is not really why character matters, but why it doesn't get the attention and respect it warrants. Character is not something that you have or don't have. All of us have character, but the key is the depth of your personality. This will enable us to lead and holistically inspire people to become the best versions of themselves.

7. PSEUDO INSPIRATIONAL LEADERSHIP

> Leadership is based on inspiration, not domination; on cooperation, not intimidation.
> - William Arthur Wood

O nce in a while, you come across an individual in a leadership position that appears to be genuine on the surface, but when you get to know this individual further, you have this funny feeling in your gut. You feel a sense of deception to the extent that you fear surrendering full loyalty to that individual. If you already did, you quickly retract your commitment and instead resort to a reclusive mode when working with this individual.

If you ever have this feeling, you are not alone. Many leaders on the surface appear to be interested in their team success and sincerely dedicated to seeing those beneath them, not only achieve organizational objectives but also reach their fullest potential in all their endeavours. In many ways, they appear to captivate and embody the characteristics of a true and inspirational leader, but their real qualities slowly emerge over time. **Inspirational leadership can be a sharp double-edged sword, with a potential immoral and unethical dimension that could be**

exploited by an unscrupulous leader inflicted on naive and unsuspecting followers, according to Air Force Colonel Mark Homrig.

Hitler, who appealed to the German people's values, was charismatic, offered a transcendent vision, and frequently encouraged his followers. However, his goal led to ruin rather than the betterment of his followers. Another example of negative inspirational leadership was Jim Jones of the People's Temple. He was very charismatic, and expressed a lofty vision that eventually led to the murder-suicide of over 800 followers in 1978, according to the PBS documentary, "Jonestown -- The Life and Death of People's Temple."

Their original charisma and go-to attitude elicit adoration among followers, who felt their leaders was a superior role model. Like various scenarios, people are drawn to such individuals because they offer new and exciting ideas in which everyone wants to be involved. Interestingly enough, most of these leaders started with a bang but ultimately fell apart after people became wise to the outrageousness of their behavior and actions. It is hard to imagine how one person can convince so many individuals to be so hateful, but such is the pull of an inspirational leader with the wrong intentions.

Inspirational leaders are often charismatic individuals, "but are not as narcissistic as pure Charismatic Leaders, who succeed through a belief in themselves rather than a belief in others," according to ChangingMinds.org. It is taken for granted that charismatic leaders are inspirational, but nothing can be further from the truth. Although all inspirational leaders have some form of charisma, not all these leaders use their gifts for noble intentions. Traditionally, an inspirational leader has been synonymous with a charismatic leader, according to the Bailey Group. After all, it's that charisma that served as the see/touch/feel of an outstanding leader. The kind of man or woman who excited his or her followers with passion, ambition, and exuberance.

That ability to work a crowd into a froth by articulating such an exciting vision of the future, no one questioning whether it made sense or was strategically sound. The truth is, many leaders dubbed as charismatic are not really inspirational at all. According to Gibson et al., charismatic leadership is described as the ability to influence others based on a supernatural gift and attractive powers. They have a charismatic effect on their followers to an unusually high degree, and these followers perceive the leader's beliefs as correct and accept him or her without questions.

Inspirational leaders, on the other hand, are leadership styles in which the leader identifies the needed change, creates a vision to guide the change through inspiration, and executes the change with the commitment of the group members. Inspirational leaders balance charisma with collaboration, confidence with virtue, and influence with transparency. **With this approach, the leader identifies a collective vision and purpose that a group can recognize and gets excited about. Ideas take precedence, rather than the leader themselves.**

How Do You Know A Genuine Leader From A Pseudo Inspirational Leadership? Look For These 5 Signs

Leaders with hidden agendas always surface when they see no value in helping others that don't show promise to provide them with immediate returns. Their counterfeit attempts to simulate caring for subordinates often get exposed, and their real agenda is revealed. What are the signs? Here's what you should be looking for as outlined by Dr. Bill Donahue.

1) **Self-advancement.** This is easy to assess. When a leader cares more about growing their platform instead of helping others build theirs, it is a tell-tale sign.

2) **Decision-making is always pragmatic.** What works for the leader transcends what is best for the team or the organization.

3) **Ethical standards are compromised.** This may be overt or subtle or even done out of ignorance, or the speed in making a decision. Nonetheless, it is a sign that things are bad. Employees or team members are treated with condescension or ignored, shortcuts are taken, and due diligence is ignored. Compliance issues in HR or legal matters are given lip service.

4) **Strategy takes priority over relationship.** In other words, regardless of the damage a decision or path may do to the team, as long as we "win" or "realize the vision" or can say "mission accomplished," the collateral relational damage is chalked up, as the cost of doing business.

5) **Everything has a price tag.** These leaders believe they can "buy" everything – trust, votes, loyalty, performance, followers, relationships, customers, members, silence, and compliance with their demands. Often money, severance packages (hush money, in some cases), promotions, perks, and other "incentives" are used to move people and strategy in the direction the leader desires – even out of the organization.

When you hear and see people continually promote themselves as leaders, frequently touting their accomplishments, pointing everything back to themselves, you are seeing someone who is about self-aggrandizement. Self-aggrandizers have an exaggerated and unsubstantiated view of their achievements and their contributions. They are legends in their minds. They are entirely self-absorbed, and everything they say and do is from a "the world revolves around me" perspective. The prominent words in their vocabularies are I, my, and me.

They also believe that they are unfairly treated and under-recognized by everyone else, primarily because, in their delusional, self-important opinions, everyone else is too ignorant and too blind to see how great and awesome they are. Followers who fear their leaders are unlikely to challenge what their leaders say or think; since he/she expect implicitly. Besides, these fake leaders neither genuinely seek nor truly accept the input of followers. They control information and resources, use their power to keep followers in a subservient position. When they do seek opinions and ideas from followers, it is usually for impression management purposes.

On the other hand, genuine leaders:
•Envision a more desirable future

•Seeks consensus and is empathic

•Respects differences and develops independent followers

•Unites through internalization of mission and values

•Is self-sacrificing and trustworthy

Inspirational leaders inspire people to believe that the impossible is possible, create change in individuals and social systems through a collective vision, and work more to better the organization and their people. Their intention is always to improve. Nelson Mandela, Mother Teresa, Martin Luther King Jr., Indra Nooyi of Pepsi, for example, all have those characteristics.

Inspirational leaders can capture people's attention effortlessly, and influence the lives of many people. It is an effective way to elicit change and get things accomplished by enlisting your people's help. Still, the leaders' intentions are the problem, which results in the negative side of inspirational leadership.

8. THE 10 MAJOR CAUSES OF FAILURE IN LEADERSHIP

THE STRONGEST
PEOPLE ARE NOT
THOSE WHO SHOW
STRENGTH IN
FRONT OF US, BUT
THOSE WHO WIN
BATTLES WE KNOW
NOTHING ABOUT.

In 1937, Napoleon Hill wrote his book 'Think and Grow Rich.' as a personal development and self-improvement book. This book is a must-read for anyone who aspires to great leadership. The philosophies in this book are really eye-opening, and it can help anyone succeed in any line of work, regardless of their location, gender, ethnicity, or social standing.

It is absolutely one of the best books I ever read, but what was surprising is the fact that the principles of leadership outlined in this book are so applicable in 2019. I want to share the ten major causes of failure in leadership with you, as described by Hill. The fact that these failures are so apt for our generation of leaders makes this book a very fascinating read.

Inability to organize details

Efficient leadership calls for the ability to organize and to master details. No genuine leader is ever "too busy" to do anything which may be required of him/her as a leader. The successful leader must be the master of all details connected with the position. That means, of course, that he/she must acquire the habit of relegating details to capable lieutenants.

Unwillingness to render humble service

Truly great leaders are willing, when occasion demands, to perform any labor which they would ask another to complete. "The greatest among ye shall be the servant of all," is a truth that all able leaders observe and respect.

The expectation of pay for what they know instead of what they do with what that which they know

The world does not pay men/women for that which they "know." It pays them for what they 'DO' or induce others to do.

Fear of competition from followers

The leader who fears that one of his/her followers may take his position is practically sure to realize that fear sooner or later. The able leader trains understudies to whom he/she may delegate, at will, any of the details of his/her position. Only in this way, may a leader multiply their attention and prepare themselves to be at many places and give attention to many things at one time.

Lack of imagination

Without imagination, the leader is incapable of meeting emergencies and creating plans to guide his followers efficiently.

Selfishness

The leader who claims all the honor for the work of his followers is sure to be met by resentment. The really great leader, CLAIMS NONE OF THE HONORS. He/she is content to see the honors when there are any and go to his/her followers because they know that most people will work harder for commendation and recognition than they will for money alone.

Intemperance

Followers do not respect an intemperate leader. Moreover, intemperance, in any of its various forms, destroys the endurance and the vitality of all who indulges in it.

Disloyalty

Perhaps this should have come at the head of the list. The leader who is not loyal to his trust, and his associates, those above him/her, and those below them, cannot for long maintain their leadership. Disloyalty marks one as being less than the dust of the earth, and brings down on one's head, the contempt he deserves. Lack of loyalty is one of the major causes of failure in every walk of life.

The emphasis of the authority of leadership

The efficient leader leads by encouraging, and not by trying to instill fear in the hearts of his/her followers. The leader who tries to impress their followers with their "authority" comes within the category of leadership through force. If a leader is a 'REAL LEADER,' he/she will not need to advertise that fact except by their conduct, sympathy, understanding, fairness, and a demonstration that they know their job.

-

Emphasis of title

The competent leader requires no "title" to give him/her the respect of his followers. The leader who makes too much over their title generally has little else to emphasize upon. The doors to the office of the real leader are open to all who wish to enter, and their working quarters are free from formality or ostentation.

These are among the more common causes of failure in leadership. Any leader possessing these faults is sufficient to induce failure. Study the list very carefully if you're aspiring to leadership, and make sure that you are free of these faults. There must be a new era of relationship between the leader and their employees, which clearly calls for a new brand of leadership within business and industry.

Those who belong to the old school of leadership-by-force must be acutely aware that this leadership brand cannot work and will not work in this 21st century. Leadership is all about people and inspiring people to believe in themselves, believe in their gifts, believe in their dreams, and, most importantly, to help the next generation of leaders become inspirational leaders.

9. WHY 50% OF NEW MANAGERS ARE NOT READY TO BECOME INSPIRATIONAL LEADERS

> **"**
> Leadership is not about being in charge.
> Leadership is about taking care of those in your charge.
>
> - Simon Sinek

One year ago, I spoke to a Human Resources manager who indicated that his company developed and implemented a leadership development programme for all their engineers because they had severe problems leading their teams. For example, the engineers had problems with communication, building trust d motivation.

He said although the engineers were fully qualified and competent in the technical aspect of their job, they had loads of problems with their leadership skills, and there were several complaints from their team as it relates to their people skills. This got me thinking, how in heaven's name did these people become responsible for managing and leading people in the first place. In many companies, as someone indicated to me, people are promoted based on their performance. Still, nothing is done to evaluate whether that person has any leadership capabilities necessary to lead people. Some people have no people skills, cannot get along with people, cannot speak to people, and believe nothing can happen without them yet, they are "in charge" and promoted as the leader of the organization. If someone has no people skills, how do they expect to get anything done?

They cannot do everything by themselves, but you know what, they usually revert to their adage of fear and intimation. I have read many comments and emails from people who express their displeasure for their managers and their behavior toward them, as it relates to their treatment at the hands of people who have no business leading people. 95% of the comments were astonishingly similar. For example, one person indicated that they worked at a company where the office manager was very condescending and verbally abusive. The person further stated that they loved their job, but refused to take the abuse from the manager. All of the comments in one form or the other alluded to the same thing, no respect from their managers.

According to Jim Harter, Gallup's Chief Scientist, it is the rite of passage in most organizations to promote someone based on their performance on the job. So if you are very good at sales, or accounting, or any number of specialties—and stay around a long time, the next step in your progression is to be promoted to manager. But the talents that make a person successful in a previous, non-management role, are rarely the same ones that will make them excel as a manager, or as a leader.

Research shows that new managers are usually promoted without the skills needed to be good managers or leaders, and 47% of companies do not have a new supervisor training program in place to help them bridge the gap, according to Ken Blanchard. Sadly, when companies promote people into a management position and do not provide the necessary training, they end up with a host of bosses and few leaders.

Research conducted by Harvard Business School professor, Linda Hill, has found that negative patterns and habits established in a manager's first year, continues to "haunt and hobble them" for the rest of their managerial careers. As a result, 60% of new managers underperform in their first two years, according to a study by the Corporate Executive Board, resulting in increased performance gaps and employee turnover.

Here are three common reasons new managers fail and what you can do about it.

Negative self-talk

When it comes to the worst things for our mental health, constant negativity is definitely one of them, especially if you are managing or leading people. When it comes to thoughts about yourself, your self-image serves as a sieve, filtering every experience and interaction while creating a running inner dialogue. You regularly talk to yourself about all of your experiences – what you think about yourself and how you see others.

This ongoing, internal dialogue is your "self-talk," and it goes with you everywhere. When these private conversations are positive, they support you and work in your best interest. When they're negative, they're destructive and demoralizing, and as a result, it impedes your leadership abilities.

Recommendation

- Make a list of all the things that trigger self-doubt and create a strategy to mitigate these occurrences.

- Reduce your inner doubt through physical activity or other types of relaxation.

- Spend some time exploring the values and principles that you feel most strongly about and write down the important ones.

- When current strategies are not working, make the necessary changes to your plans, activities, objectives, or behavior.

Justifying your behavior and blaming others

Do you find it hard to admit when you're wrong? I read an article where the author shared his experience of a leader blaming everyone else for the way he was acting. "I sat there listening to this poor justification for unacceptable behavior thinking to myself: The excuses that people come up with never cease to amaze me." but that Theory of Cognitive Dissonance.

The feeling of discomfort caused by performing an action that is discrepant from one's self-concept, cognitive dissonance always produces discomfort. In response, many people try to reduce it by blaming others for their actions. There is no I in a team, and leadership is all about building and creating an environment that allows their people to maximize their full potential while helping the company achieve its objectives.

Recommendation

- Lead by example and encourage others in a positive way

- Validate your team by creating trust.

- Genuinely show interest in helping others.

- Admit when you are wrong

Lacking Emotional Intelligence

For leaders, having emotional intelligence is essential for success. Who is more likely to succeed, a leader who shouts at his team when he/she is under stress, or a leader who stays in control and calmly assesses the situation?

Leaders with self-control stay calm and clear-headed while under stress or during a crisis and maintain emotional balance. Leadership is demanding, and the people who can juggle multiple demands, but remain focused on a group's goals are the ones who are likely to succeed.

Recommendation

- Listen attentively to your team to understand their perspectives

- Create and maintains good working relationships with other people.

- Practice empathy, feel what other people are feeling so you can put yourself in their shoes.

- Read non-verbal cues, read messages conveyed by facial gestures, posture, eye movement, and body language.

With over two million people being promoted into their first leadership roles each year—and over 50% struggling or failing—the care and feeding of first-time managers need to be front and center on every leadership development curriculum.

Learning and development professionals must help new managers understand their role and responsibility when it comes to managing and leading people. Still, it is also super important that the company knows the specific leadership qualities they expect from someone when recruiting for a leadership position. No one should feel uncomfortable at their job, especially when you are doing something you love.

Your work should make you feel motivated and inspired to perform at your optimum best. Still, that feeling slowly fades away when you have a manager who has no clue about leading and believes everything revolves around his or her existence. When you enter into the realm of leadership, you are in the business of people. Inspiring and motivating people to get things done. You lead by example, and you are comfortable with the uncertainty that leadership can bring. As such, you are flexible in adapting to new challenges and nimble in adjusting to sudden change.

Leaders who have high standards not only for themselves but for others continually learn how to improve performance, along with their team. They see opportunities in situations where others would see a setback and lead others positively, from diverse backgrounds and cultures to create an atmosphere of respect, helpfulness, and cooperation. Leadership is about people. If you want to become an effective leader, you must draw others into an active commitment to the team's effort, build a spirit of positive relationships, and create a sense of purpose among your people.

10. ENCOURAGE YOUR EMPLOYEES TO THINK AND ACT MORE AS LEADERS

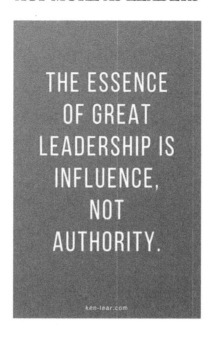

THE ESSENCE OF GREAT LEADERSHIP IS INFLUENCE, NOT AUTHORITY.

ken-lear.com

Ray Dalio, the billionaire founder of the hedge fund Bridgewater Associates, which currently has $160 billion in assets under management, got an email from one of his client advisers. The email was sent after a meeting with an important potential client, the email stated:

Ray — you deserve a "D-" for your performance today . . . you rambled for 50 minutes . . .It was obvious to all of us that you did not prepare at all because there is no way you could have and been that disorganized at the outset if you had prepared. We told you this prospect had been identified as a "must-win". . . today was really bad . . . we can't let this happen again.

Now picture you sending an email like that to your CEO or the founder of a company. Imagine his/her reaction. Rather than being offended, Dalio says the email exemplified the idea that he wanted his employees to speak up. Bridgewater Associates has a trademark policy of radical transparency.

Everyone at the company speaks their minds because Ray Dalio understands that leadership is much more than being in charge and managing people. "In order to be successful, we must have independent thinkers — so independent that they'll bet against the consensus," Dalio indicated.

I can remember a janitor sending an all-staff email at a particular company, reminding staff to place all garbage in their bins. The CEO, reading the email, was astounded that a "low level" employee, was allowed to send an email to all staff about putting trash in their bins. The CEO reacted by barring anyone from sending all staff emails without the consent from their manager.

The most effective businesses today encourages every employee to take on leadership roles. When employees become leaders, decisions are made more quickly; customers are happier, and tremendous amounts of time, energy, and money can be saved. Not only will this take some burden off your shoulders as the CEO or manager, but your employees will be happier, the gossipers will be significantly reduced, and your employees will be more engaged and effective.

In a company with a culture of leadership, all employees, not just those with "VP" or "Chief" in their titles, are expected to think and act like leaders. What separates the good leaders from the great inspirational leaders is their ability to build a culture of leadership throughout their organization that cultivates great leaders. According to Donald Hatter, if a company is genuinely concerned about creating that kind of environment, they should have a slightly different approach and a broader focus. For example, employees should spend time learning how to become more self-aware, empathetic, and motivational.

Great leaders are genuinely concerned about those they work with, which is why people want to follow them voluntarily. Every company executive should be tasked with training, mentoring, and nurturing their team on how to be future corporate executive leaders. Remember, view your employees not as who they are in their current job titles, but as who they can be with your leadership training and development. Every organization needs a great leader charting the course, but you must have leaders within your company as well.

Work should be a place where you are motivated and inspired to make a difference, "there is no way you were born just to pay bills and then die." Having people who can energize and motivate others to work together to achieve common goals is essential for your team's development and overall success of your company. No company can ever have too many employees with great leadership qualities, gone are the days when leadership was associated with fancy titles or designations only. Nowadays, leadership isn't about your title; it's about one life influencing another for the greater good of the individuals they are entrusted to serve; their customers, community, and by extension, the world.

11. THE EMPATHETIC LEADER

> "Being a leader is more than just wanting to lead. Leaders have empathy for others and a keen ability to find the best in people ... not the worst ...by truly caring for others."
>
> Henry Gruland

Can you remember the incident that took place on a United Airlines flight in 2017 where Dr. Dao was dragged off the plane, blood running from his mouth and mumbling "just kill me." Many accuse United Airlines CEO Oscar Munoz of lacking empathy towards Dr. Dao in his response after the incident calling the passenger disruptive' and 'belligerent,' which sparked a public campaign to boycott United Airlines. Munoz subsequently changes his tone and issue an apology to Dr. Dao.

However, nothing changed at United because weeks later, a United gate agent refuses to allow two young girls to board a plane because their leggings didn't adhere to the airline's dress code for "pass" travelers. Just last year, a flight attendant insisted on putting a dog in an overhead bin because its carrier wouldn't fit under the seat and assured the dog's owner that it would be fine up there. The dog was found dead upon arrival at the destination.

To continually inspire your people to perform at their optimum best, you must understand your people's perspectives, and you must give them the respect they deserve, which is reflected in the service provided to their customers. Empathy allows you to achieve this, and as a result, the most critical skill leaders need today is empathy, and the best leaders are empathetic leaders, according to Lolly Daskal. However, many people today believe that emphatic leaders are weak. For some reason, they think that this "soft Skill" is a nonessential variable that adds no value to their leadership and, by extension, their organization when all the studies have link empathy to superior business results according to Bruna Martinuzz.

"Can you teach someone to be empathetic?" We all know some people who are naturally and consistently empathetic – these are the people who can easily forge positive connections with others, according to Bruna. They are people who use empathy to engender trust and build bonds; they are catalysts who can create positive communities for the greater good. However, even if empathy does not come naturally to some of us, I firmly believe that we can develop this capacity.

Here are a few practical tips you should consider to help become an emphatic leader as outline by Martinuzz:

Take A Personal Interest In Your People

When a leader demonstrates to employees that they care, the reciprocity reaction kicks in, to the point where they put more effort into helping their leader. By extension, their organization becomes successful, according to Harvey Deutschendorf. Successful organizations are aware of this, and their leaders continuously look for ways to notice, compliment, and find ways to show their appreciation to their staff. Show people that you care and ask them questions about their hobbies, challenges, families, and aspirations. This genuine curiosity about their lives will help foster a great, long-lasting relationship.

Listening Skills.

To understand others and sense what they are feeling, leaders must be good listeners. Skilled listeners let others know that they are being heard, and they express an understanding of concerns and problems. When a leader is a good listener, people feel respected, and trust can grow.

Be Fully Present

Don't check your email, look at your watch or take phone calls when a direct report drops into your office to talk to you. Truly engage your people and create meaningful connections. Put yourself in their shoes. How would you feel if someone did that to you?

Encourage and Develop Your People

Particularly the quiet ones, when they speak up in meetings. A simple thing like an attentive nod can boost people's confidence.

Culture

Leaders live their purpose by serving others and continually inspiring their team to lift the organization to higher performance levels. Leaders, especially people who are new to formal leadership, must understand that a leaders' role is to create a culture that allows their people to become the very best version of themselves, which will automatically result in added value to their organization.

Inspiration

Without inspiration, you cannot lead, you will be able to manage, but you cannot call yourself a leader. Leadership and inspiration are inseparable; you cannot expect great performances from your team if they are not inspired. You cannot expect great products or excellent service from your staff if they are not motivated by a leader who lives and breathes the organization's purpose, values, and vision every day.

Lead By Example

Leaders are most potent when they lead by example, but some people have no people skills, cannot get along with people, cannot speak to people, and cannot build relationships to save their lives. However, for some strange reason, these are the people who are elevated into a leadership position with no type of mentoring, training, or coaching.

Empathy is a vital part of emotional intelligence that several researchers believe is critical to being an effective leader. Some companies believe that empathy is so essential that they send managers to "empathy training." According to the Wall Street Journal, 20% of employers now offer empathy training, which is up substantially from 10 years prior. Empathy helps build a great team, build trust, and nurture a new generation of leaders.

As I mentioned before, with over two million people being promoted into their first leadership roles each year—and over 50% struggling or failing—the care and feeding of first-time managers need to be front and center on every leadership development curriculum. Learning and development professionals must help new managers understand their role and responsibility when it comes to managing and leading people. However, it's also super important that the company knows the specific leadership qualities they expect from someone when recruiting for a leadership position.

Many people are promoted or recruited into a leadership position without understanding the fundamental philosophy of leadership; **It's all about people!** The talents that make a person successful in a previous, non-management role are rarely the same ones that will make them excel as a manager or as a leader, according to retired four-star general Colin Powell. Leadership is all about people, not plans or strategies, but people; motivating and inspiring people to believe in something beyond their self-limitations to achieve a result that benefits and adds value to themselves, their company, and the people they serve.

Whether you're the leader of a small team, the manager of a large retail store, or the CEO of a global corporation, your people make your organization successful. Oh, and by the way, previous reports say that United Airlines reached a confidential settlement with Dr. Dao to the tune of $140 million for the injuries he suffered, including a broken nose, a concussion, and broken teeth.

It pays to show empathy.

12. LEAD YOUR TEAM BY EXAMPLE

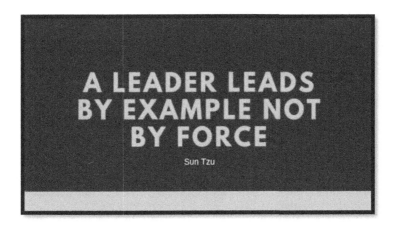

T here's hardly anything worse for a company's morale, according to Bruna Martinuzzi than leaders who practice the "Do as I say, not as I do" philosophy. For example, the manager who tells everyone to stay late and finish the project, but leaves promptly at 5:00 pm to golf. Or the CEO who criticizes everyone for spending time on the internet, but is discovered buying groceries online in the middle of the afternoon, or the CFO who recommends layoffs to stop "unnecessary spending," but buys brand-new luxury office furniture.

Most leaders know that their actions can influence how a team feels and performs. Moreover, **when leaders don't practice what they preach, you can almost see the staff's loss of enthusiasm and goodwill.** It's like watching the air go out of a balloon – and cynicism and disappointment usually take its place. Take Satya Nadella, for instance, since taking over as CEO of Microsoft, Satya's first order of business was dedicated to changing the culture of the company and leading the change by example. It's a fascinating turnaround of a company that allowed itself to be bog down with infighting and win at all costs, but the change was worth it.

Satya Nadella Approach.

Microsoft invested significant resources in robotics and even introduced Tay, a teenage girl-inspired bot that had been programmed to interact with Twitter users. I don't know if you guys are familiar with the story. According to the Financial Times, within hours of activating her on the social media sites, Tay was parroting racist, misogynistic and pornographic lines that other users prompted her to repeat. Microsoft rapidly grounded the objectionable bot with a statement that said it was "deeply sorry for the unintended offensive and hurtful tweets from Tay."

The experiments with Tay was a PR disaster for Microsoft, but Mr. Nadella dealt with it empathetically. He emailed the Microsoft team behind Tay, the artificial intelligence researchers, software engineers, and improv comedians — the morning after Tay was neutralized. He made sure the team did not feel bad for actually taking the risk. That's huge. According to Mr. Nadella, "you've got to make sure that if you make mistakes, you learn from them." This encapsulates the management style of the 49-year-old chief executive — frank, decisive, and forgiving. Mr. Nadella is modeling the behavior he expects at Microsoft.

It's a significant shift for Microsoft. Microsoft had become a company where teams had to compete for resources and ideas that were perhaps in the best interests of the company as a whole but often lost out because it didn't suit the interests of a particular executive or team.

When Mr. Nadella took over, he wholeheartedly embraced a one Microsoft vision and went about ensuring the change was embodied across various levels of the company. Under Mr. Nedella's leadership, Microsoft stock jumped from $200B in value to more than $492B in October of 2016, the company's shares surged past its all-time high price of $59.56.

Seemingly overnight, the company was back with a vengeance, removing the perception of Borg Microsoft, the bullying juggernaut that ruled the software industry with an iron fist? Remember the Microsoft under Bill Gates and Steve Ballmer mocking Linux, calling it cancer, laughing at the iPhone. Or when Ballmer dismissed Android as too hard to use (a billion Android phones shipped last year.) The new Microsoft has shed its arrogance, and you can thank Satya Nadella for it. What I particularly admired about this situation with Tay was the fact that Mr.

Nadella took the time to email everyone on the team; I can only imagine what the team felt when they got that email from the CEO. As the leader of your company, you wield tremendous influence, and as a result, your every move is monitored, and your every word is analyzed. So you have to be particularly aware of your behavior. What you give off will influence the culture of your company. Mr. Nadella gets it, but unfortunately, many don't. I can remember a father telling his son, "do as I say but not as I do." You all ever heard that statement, ridiculous as it sounds. That's what many CEOs are doing at their companies—creating a total contradiction between their words and their actions, which usually causes confusion and mistrust among their employees.

If you're in a leadership position, then you know that you have a responsibility to your team to lead by example. No matter what the situation is, you have that responsibility; if double standards exist and the leader is saying one thing and then doing another, it always feels like a betrayal. If this ever happened to you, you can probably remember that sense of disappointment and letdown. The legendary Jack Welch, according to Bruna Martinuzzi, turned GE upside down. By developing a "boundaryless organization," a place where everyone is free to brainstorm and think of ideas – instead of waiting for someone "higher up," in the bureaucracy to think of them first.

He wanted his team turned loose, and he promised to listen to ideas from anyone in the company. And he did. Everyone from the lowest line workers to senior managers got his attention – if they had something to say or a new idea that might make the company better. It wasn't just talking, and it didn't take his team long to figure that out. Welch stayed true to his passions, his commitment, and led by example. GE became an incredibly successful company under his leadership, and his team was always willing to follow his lead because the people within knew that he always kept his word. As a leader, part of your job is to inspire the people around you to push themselves – and, in turn, the company to greatness.

To develop yourself into a great leader, you must set the tone and lead by example. When leaders don't 'practice what they preach,' it can be almost impossible for a team to work together successfully. How can anyone trust a leader who talks about one thing, but does another? Leading by example is the most potent form of leadership. Effective and inspirational leaders model the way for others to follow.

Great leaders push their people forward with excitement, inspiration, trust, and vision. To become one of the great leaders, it takes the strength of character and a firm commitment to do the right thing, at the right time, for the right reason. This means doing what you say when you say it. Become the kind of leader that people would follow voluntarily, even if you had no title or position. If your team can't trust you and your character is questionable, you'll never lead your people and, by extension, your company to greatness.

13. ARE YOU A LEADER OR A MANAGER?

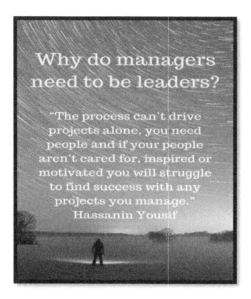

There is a continuing controversy about the difference between leadership and management. There are several conclusions to be drawn from this debate. However, one thing is absolutely clear, **not all managers exercise leadership, and many people who called themselves "a leader" cannot lead, manage maybe, but lead, no.** Organizations provide their managers with legitimate authority to lead, but there is no assurance that they will lead effectively. As a manager, you are the de facto leader, but what prevents the manager from becoming a leader is their qualities.

For example, if you are quite contented to focus on planning and budgeting, organizing and staffing, controlling, and problem-solving, you will get honors as an average manager. However, if you add some leadership qualities in that mix, for instance:

- Accepting and learning from failure

- Purpose and values-driven

- Communication

- Emotional intelligence

- Inspirationally motivating

- Visionary

- Listening

- Leading by example

- Empowering others

- Self- development

Wow! When you add those qualities, you will become one hell of an inspirational leader! Some people think it's a fallacy; this type of leadership cannot exist in the real world. Still, many organizations are led by inspirational leaders who embody these qualities. For example, Glassdoor's highest-rated CEOs for 2018, listed some of the most outstanding CEOs in the world that exemplified what leadership is all about.

The highest-rated CEO for 2018 is Eric S. Yuan, from Zoom Video Communications; Yuan got an employees' approval rating of 99%, the

100th rank CEO Kevin A. Lobo, got an employees' approval rating of 90%. The list comprised of:

- Michael F. Mahoney from Boston Scientific

- Mark Zuckerberg from Facebook

- Jeff Weiner from LinkedIn

- James Downing from St, Jude Children's Hospital

- Marc Benioff from Salesforce

- Colleen Wegman from Wegman Food Markets

And many, many more great CEOs who believed and lived the values of their companies. More importantly, they recognized that their employees are their most prized resource and genuinely care about their people's needs. The Great Place To Work Institute, together with Fortune published the 100 Best Companies to Work For every year. When you read the reviews from these companies, it is incredible how people feel so inspired and motivated to work. Their employee turnover rate is close to zero, and their employees are fiercely loyal to their leader and the company, **Why? Great leadership.**

In today's dynamic workplace, organizations need inspirational leadership and active management for optimal effectiveness. We need leaders to challenge the status quo, to inspire and to motivate. But moreover, we also require managers to assist in developing and maintaining a smoothly functioning workplace. Still, they should also have strong leadership skills to maintain a positive work environment as well. Many of the problems existing in varying organizations today come from piss poor leadership and management. While great leaders encourage their employees to reach their full potential and help their organizations surpass their goals, weak managers push their employees away to the point where many of them jump ship.

According to the Wall Street Journal, nearly half of the employees who leave jobs do so to get away from their bosses. As such, if you don't want to lose your best employees, it's critical that you do everything you can to ensure you fill managerial positions with the right people in the first place. The success of any organization comes from team members who challenge the "but that is how we do it here" refrain. According to John Couris, top-performing team members are those who possess the confidence to challenge the status quo, think strategically, and speak up to put the organization's success at the front of every decision.

It makes absolutely no sense to recruit the best and tell them what to do if you are the leader, you should not be the smartest person in the room. According to Michael Dell, try never to be the most intelligent person in the room. And if you are, I suggest you invite smarter people ... or find a different room. You can't grow as a leader unless you have the brightest and most innovative people in your corner. Leaders don't need to have all the answers; no one is an expert in everything – not even you.

When you develop that type of culture within your organization, and you are not an insecure leader who believed everyone should agree with everything you say or do, you are nurturing and developing the next generation of leaders. Couris further argued that leading a successful organization is developing a team that enables members to contribute to the best of their ability. By surrounding yourself with smart and driven folks, which can be smart and motivated - you will develop a culture that yields a great deal of success.

To successfully navigate all the disruptions in today fiercely competitive world, we are going to need a new generation of purpose-driven leaders, who can inspire people to believe that the impossible is possible, to believe that they can achieve the unimaginable, to challenge their people to be the best while helping them develop their skills and competence. We need leaders to stand up for their employees, to lead by example, and to create an environment; their employees will love to come too; when you achieve that! Your organization will attract the best and the brightest, and become one of the best companies to work for in the world.

14. INSPIRE PURPOSE NOT PROFIT

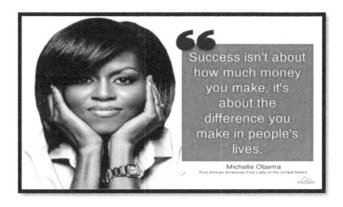

When most of your employees believe the primary purpose of their organization is to make money, the organization is destined for mediocrity. In Robert E. Quinn and Anjan V. Thakor's article in the Harvard Business Review, they shared a story of Gerry Anderson when he first became the president of DTE Energy.

At the height of the recession in 2008, Gerry Anderson required his people to reach for something more beside their own self targets and preservation, but deep in his heart, he knew his people were not inspired. In a survey conducted at the company, the results show that DTE employees' were not very engaged. According to the article, employees couldn't seem to break free of old, tired behaviors; they weren't bringing their smarts and creativity to their jobs, and they weren't performing up to their potential. What turn things around! The new leader infused the core purpose of the company in the everyday lives' of each employee. Before the recession, Anderson considered purpose as empty and simplistic rhetoric. Having run into a dead-end in figuring out how to make his own organization thrive,

Anderson was reexamining some of his underlying assumptions about management. He was open to what a purpose-driven organization can do to inspire his team.

Anderson made a video that articulated his employees' higher purpose. It showed DTE's truck drivers, plant operators, corporate leaders, and many others on the job. It described the impact of their work on the well-being of the community—the factory workers, teachers, and doctors who needed the energy DTE generated. The first group of professional employees to see the video gave it a standing ovation. When union members viewed it, some were moved to tears. Never before had their work been framed as a meaningful contribution to the greater good. The video brought to life DTE's new statement of purpose: "We serve with our energy, the lifeblood of communities and the engine of progress."

One must remember that a higher purpose is not about economic exchanges; it reflects something more aspirational. It explains how the people involved with an organization are making a difference, providing a sense of meaning, and drawing support for the organization's vision, mission, and objectives. Most of all, it builds trust, and everyone has a shared sense of purpose in the organization.

It should be noted that when we talk about an inspiring purpose, we are not talking about those boring mission statements that no one in the company can recite. We are talking about a crisp and clear cause that unites and activates all people within the organization. An inspiring mission that does best for the organization, the employees, the customers, and the world in the long-term. According to Markus Heinen, Chief Innovation Officer of EY, "Purpose is an aspirational reason for being grounded in humanity and inspires action." In other words, an organization needs to stand for something it believes in, going beyond profit and impacting society. This can, of course, extend beyond pure social projects. If a company can direct its vision, mission, and business model towards something that creates purpose, and can demonstrate how their products create purpose; it is even stronger.

"Purpose led companies generates significant revenue"

The Game Changers 500, list companies that are defined as 'For Benefit as oppose to For-Profit.' They rank companies based on their business acumen to make the world a better place. Many of these companies are very, very successful, making loads of profits and adding tons of values to their employees, community, and customers daily. Let's look at two companies from the list Itaipu Binacional and Vancity.

Itaipu Binacional

Itaipu Binacional is the world's largest hydroelectric power plant located at the Brazilians and Paraguayans point to a river stretch known as Itaipu. The exploration of renewable alternative energy sources was conceptualized as a means to ensure a robust development for Brazil and Paraguay, which coincided with the emergence of the worldwide crisis precipitated by the increase in oil prices. In the year 2000, the company generated 93.4 billion kilowatt-hours of electricity. It celebrated 20 years in operation with enough power to supply the world for 36 days, in 2017, Itaipu made 96.4 million MWh of electricity, which is the fourth largest annual production volume achieved by the plant since its inauguration. Itaipu's has committed a lot of their resources to effectively contributing to the sustainable development of influential areas in Brazil and Paraguay. Over 5000 students have benefited from the company training programmes, and the company generated 3.7 Billion USD in revenue in 2012.

Vancity

In 1946, 14 residents of Vancouver established the Vancouver City Savings Credit Union to provide financial services to regular folks, who were unable to get financial assistance. By 1990, Vancity's assets reach $2 billion, and the Vancity Community Foundation was established with a $1 million endowment to enrich the community through a co-operative version of philanthropy. Now, Vancity is one of the world's leading value-based banks with over 17 billion in assets, and the largest organization in Canada to adopt the Living Wage policy. They were recognizing the social and economic benefits of paying employees a wage that meets their basic living needs.

Great companies think differently, and great companies recognize the importance of using social logic to grow and inspire their people. These companies became more than a place to make money. Purpose-led companies usually have strong employee engagement. When people are inspired by something much bigger than their own self-preservation, great things happen. As the leader, give your people a purpose they are willing to die for, instead of coming to work for 5, 10, or 20 years doing the same mundane task every day, without any sense of direction.

The organization's vision and mission are critical for enabling others to feel as if their work has a purpose and meaning beyond the tasks they perform each day. Those without this higher calling often require lots of external motivation to keep moving forward. Those that operate and live from a place of purpose are inspired every day to give 100%. They may get tired, but they can reach back to their higher purpose to be inspired. Leaders must help their staff connect the dots by explaining the big picture to all. Communicating the big picture regularly will help reinforce the reason your organization exists. To remain relevant in today's business landscape, companies have to be more than just instruments for generating money. Companies need to recognize the impact their business can have on the lives of many people. When you inspired purpose in every nook and cranny of the organization, your employees will feel inspired every day and perform at heights you never imagine.

15. INSPIRATIONAL LEADERS INSPIRE GREAT CULTURES

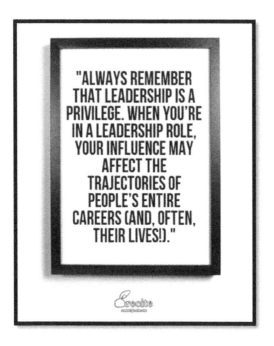

"ALWAYS REMEMBER THAT LEADERSHIP IS A PRIVILEGE. WHEN YOU'RE IN A LEADERSHIP ROLE, YOUR INFLUENCE MAY AFFECT THE TRAJECTORIES OF PEOPLE'S ENTIRE CAREERS (AND, OFTEN, THEIR LIVES!)."

T wo incidents took place in 2018 that disturbed me tremendously, and from the look of it, they are not one-off incidents. In the first instance, I was waiting to cash some items I picked up at the supermarket. One of the supervisors stopped one of the guys on the floor and said to him, in full view of everyone in the waiting area, "how could you forget the stuff I ask you for, you don't use your brain." I felt pretty awful for the guy because the tone the lady use was disgusting, and anyone looking on could see the embarrassed look on his face.

The following day I stopped to buy a box of chicken and chips for my babysitter. While waiting, I noticed the young lady at the counter; I have this habit of observing my surroundings, especially when it comes to watching people and their interactions with other people. The young lady at the counter said to the manager, "excuse me I need to go for lunch I have been waiting for a long time," the manager shouted, "well go"; shouted! I was utterly shocked, and I asked myself, how in heaven's name, someone with that type of attitude can become responsible for people.

It was disturbing, especially for someone who believes in employees' well-being, inspiration, motivation, and emotional intelligence. One can deduce that these people are not being mentored to lead, and are not given the necessary training to lead, and have absolutely no people skills. But do you know what is even more disturbing, many people believe this type of behavior is standard. Typical for their manager to verbally abuse them, normal to work in an environment of distrust and deceit, or to engage in gossip or to look for self-preservation at the expense of everything and everyone.

This is not normal.

Many of these managers expect, and in many instances, demand respect from their direct reports as if it is some form of entitlement. Great leaders don't demand respect; they don't have too; people will naturally follow them because of their leadership skills and ability to inspire and motivate people. What makes some companies great? What is that magic formula these companies used to get their employees excited about their work? Most firms attract and retain the best talent available, and in many instances, the turnover rate in many of these companies are close to zero. I read several comments from many employees from various companies, and I must admit their expression and descriptions of their workplace were very, very inspirational. For example, take this quote from an employee from **Zappos**.

"It's not every day that you wake up and look forward to going to work. I couldn't always say that about past jobs, but it's something I can definitely say about working at Zappos. The people, the energy, and the culture at Zappos all make work not even feel like work. Time has flown by since I joined the company, and I've loved every minute of it."

Why all organizations cannot have an organizational culture that gets you excited about your job, work should not be a prison sentence, waiting for bail every day at 4 or 5 in the afternoon. We spend so much of our time at our place of work; it should be a natural extension of our home, and I believe in all my heart that every organization should be a great place to work.

All of the great companies have similar traits. Their most significant strength is their culture and the ability for leadership to develop, maintain, and retain their unique culture over the company's life. It is refreshing to listen and read about companies who tried to make their workplace the best, and the icing on the cake; increased profit as a result of a great culture. If you are a skeptic, do your own research. But, the fantastic thing, money is not the prime motivator for many of these employees. They are not obsessed with only generating profit. Many of these employees love the family-like spirit in their organization and a shared purpose that keeps them motivated and inspired to perform at their best.

All of these companies, such as Silent Rivers, SAP, Salesforce, Google, Netflix, Squaremouth, and Boston Scientific, all have a deep-seated awareness of their values and implement strategies to generate a high level of employee engagement. This emotional commitment means engaged employees actually care about their work and their company. They don't work just for a paycheque, or just for the next promotion, but work on behalf of the organization's goals and a strong belief in its purpose.

When employees care—when they are engaged—they use discretionary effort. This means the engaged computer programmer works overtime when needed, without being asked. This means the engaged retail clerk picks up the trash on the store floor, even if the boss isn't watching. This means the TSA's agent will pull a suspicious bag to be searched, even if it's the last bag on their shift. When you generate that type of culture of treating your people with respect and dignity while recruiting your employees based on your organizational culture. Committing to the corporate values, having open communication on all fronts of your company, and creating a culture of trust, when you create that kind of environment, you have created something so special, only a few companies have mastered.

When you create that kind of environment, you will witness significant growth in your employees personally and professionally. If a manager has no respect for his/her team, how can you expect any respect in return? They will follow their instructions because of their position on the org chart, but they will not support them voluntarily, and all trust will be lost. When all trust is broken down, a company can never function at an optimum level; the company will experience a high

16. ARE YOU TREATING YOUR TEAM WITH RESPECT

When employees respect
each other and get along
in the workplace, it's
amazing how productivity
increases, morale
increases and employees
are more courteous to
customers.

QUOTEHD.COM   Maureen Wild

J eff got the job he dreamed about, the vice-president of R&D in a new company. Jeff was eager to take this job because of the corner office, an executive assistant, and a fancy title, but what empower Jeff more was the fact that he can now order people around, and within a couple of weeks, Jeff made his mark.

On a Tuesday afternoon a mere fortnight into his tenure, Jeff sent an email out to the team of 30 or so developers with crystal clear instructions. "Everyone stays late tonight. No excuses. The projects are behind schedule." That was it. Additional context remained elusive. Fearful for their jobs, all team members complied. There were no further instructions, new assignments, or emails from the boss. Confusion reigned. Everyone just continued coding. At 8 p.m., a couple of the developers ordered pizza for the group. By 9:30 p.m., one of the team leaders approached the vice-president who had remained in his office.

"Jeff, you asked us to stay late. It's now at 9:30 p.m. Is there anything else you wanted us specifically to do? Because we'd all like to go home now." Jeff replied, "It was a test. I just wanted to see where people's loyalty lay. They're free to go home now." Unsurprisingly, Jeff's lack of concern for his team members' personal lives backfired once word got out about his antics. A third of the developers left the company within a few weeks, and six months later, Jeff was terminated from his vice-president role. He couldn't take the corner office with him.

I read this story from Dan Pontefract's article. It's Okay To Be A Leader And Treat Team Members With Respect, and I immediately thought to myself how these people become responsible for people. Is it that people are recruited into a leadership role with no assessment of their ability to lead? This is primarily why great companies have rigorous recruitment processes because the person who has that enormous leadership responsibility has the influence to change the trajectory of people's lives, which will directly impact the organization's ability to achieve its purpose.

Always treat your people with respect; **if you are a leader, your first task is to care for your team. Treating people like objects or failing to be humane is not leadership; instead, it's telling signs of a dictator, according to Dan Pontefract.** One must remember that respect is not an entitlement; it's earned. First, you have to give respect to receive respect, and you must treat all of your employees fairly, and express the value you have for them. Listen to your team when they come to you with their ideas or concerns, and never talk down to them or insult them. In short, respect is not an entitlement; it is something you earn as a leader; you must first give respect to receive it.

Listen to your team opinions; show your team that you are genuinely listening. Nothing is more disrespectful than speaking to someone, and they are showing you that they are not listening. It's the ultimate form of disrespect. As the leader, check your ego at the door. Be aware of your tone, body language, expression, and demeanor during all interactions. Some people can detect the slightest hints of what seems like disrespect, even if you aren't aware of it yourself.

According to a survey conducted by the Society for Human Resources Management (SHRM), respectful treatment of all employees at all levels was rated as "very important" by 72 percent of those surveyed, making it the top contributor to overall employee job satisfaction. To earn your team's trust, leaders must build and sustain respectful workplaces because employees are inclined to work harder, be more inspired, and stay productive. Employees report more conflicts in workplaces with little or no respect for their team.

Recognize that, like you, your co-workers, reports, and superiors have rights, opinions, wishes, experience, and competence. They also make mistakes, which are simply lessons to be learned. They have similar concerns and insecurities and share the common goal of wanting to perform their jobs successfully. Respect in the workplace breeds a healthy and high trust work environment. A professional, respectful work culture encourages productivity and growth. The staff works optimally, knowing they are valued and respected for their ideas as well as their role within the company. Jeff proves that the opposite is also true if the leader shows no respect for their team, the organization will become toxic, trust will be eroded, the best people will leave, and the organization will eventually become irrelevant.

17. FAITH OR FEAR

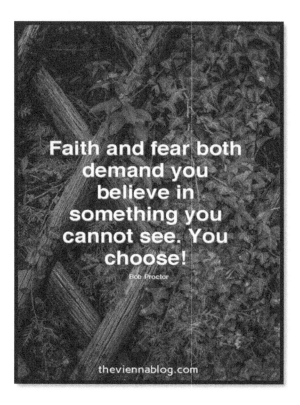

Faith and fear both demand you believe in something you cannot see. You choose!

Bob Proctor

theviennablog.com

O ur society today is driven by our minds, our fears and our ego according to Connie Chapman. We do not place as much value and emphasis on passion, love, fulfillment, and spiritual purpose. Instead, we are driven by fear to remain safe and to get the approval of people we think have our best interest at heart. **To become an inspirational leader, you must have a deep-seated love for your work, you must do something that you love, you must become a master of your craft, and you must have a strong relationship with**

faith. An inspirational leader is passionate about their vision and mission of their organization because they understand that their passion and love for their work, enable others to feel passionate as well. Shared passion makes organizations soar, according to Susan M. Heathfield. It is so important to follow your heart and pursue something you love to do despite failure and challenges. You must believe everything will work out at the end.

When Jeff Bezos decided to leave his high paying Vice President job to start a company, no one ever heard of; everyone told him he was crazy. But Bezo was unfulfilled at that job, and you cannot lead people if you are not inspired; you may be able to manage them, but you cannot lead them. So he formed his own company; it was difficult at the start just like any other start-up, but he believed his company would one day make it big, his faith was so great he was willing to bet against popular opinion to pursue something he loved. Bezo followed his heart, found his love, and went for it.

"Those who are crazy enough to think they can change the world usually do." Steve Jobs

If you try something and it doesn't work out, that's ok too, keep trying. I listen to an interview with T.D. Jakes and Steven Furtick. In the interview, T.D Jakes shared a story about his son, who was pursuing an engineering degree in Music and had concerns about his purpose. T.D. Jakes son said "dad, suppose I throw everything at it, and it's really not the thing I want to do," and T.D Jakes replied, "don't worry about it son, if it is not the thing, it will be the thing that leads to the thing."

Everything in life is connected; every experience is a preparation for the thing you were destined to become. As a leader, your team will feed off of you, Richard Branson identifies the ability to inspire as the single most critical leadership skill. The ability to infuse energy, passion, commitment, connection, and faith to an organization's mission and direction is essential in any growing company. When we are filled with inspiration, we often don't need external motivation to move forward. The feeling of purpose and meaning is enough to propel us.

If you are going through the motions with no sense of direction and purpose, your team will sense it. If you are filled with fear, with paralysis for trying anything new, people will not follow you voluntarily; they may because of your title and your position on the org chart, but if they have a choice, they would not. Your team will draw their inspiration from you, so it is imperative you love what you do, our life is already hectic, especially if you have a family. You have to get the kids ready for school, in some instances dropping and picking up from school, doing homework, putting the kids to bed, and trying to find some time for yourself, and with your significant other wow! It can be exhausting at times. But what is, even more, draining on your health, is staying in a job you hate and convincing yourself that no other options exist.

We both know the world is overflowing with opportunities, but you have such a fear of failure that you decided to stay in your comfort zone, coming up with all kinds of excuses. If you fear failure as a leader, your comfort zone will give you all the reasons to settle for a life far below your God-given potential.

Take a minute for a second, really, take a second, relax your body, let your mind wander a bit, let your mind loose; what is that thing you want to do, but for some reason, you are holding yourself back. Forget about what your coworkers may think, or your mother or your father, or people in general; this is your life, and you must live your life happily, fulfilled, and to the fullest.

As a leader your team will feed off of you, your team will draw their inspiration from you, so don't hold yourself back, follow your heart, because when you do, you automatically give people the confidence to go after their dreams.

18. REMEMBER YOUR WHY

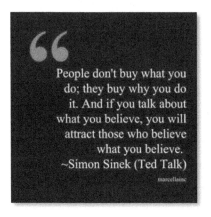

People don't buy what you do; they buy why you do it. And if you talk about what you believe, you will attract those who believe what you believe.
~Simon Sinek (Ted Talk)

Four years ago, my wife and I decided to build our dream home. Our family was growing, and we outgrew our current home. We were so excited because we got all the plans drawn up, we carefully designed the house; we knew which paint for each room, we created the layout; we went all out because this was our dream home, something we were dreaming about for a long time.

Construction got started, work was going smoothly, but unfortunately, we were faced with some severe challenges. At that time, our local cement company in Trinidad and Tobago was not producing cement because of a strike by their employees, and as a result, the price of cement increased by 100% overnight. Added to that, we ran into some financial challenges that totally erase all of our budgets, and we stopped construction on the house my wife, and I dreamt about for so long. It was a significant disappointment at that time, and I blame myself for it, and I lost all excitement. I lost me and my why, while in the process, losing all inspiration to deal with the challenges of continuing to build our new home.

To become an inspiration to your team, to your family, to yourself, you must remember your why. Remember why you choose this career, this house, this car, your spouse, your job, this strategy, these objectives, or this location. We must know our purpose, and when those challenging times come and believe me they will come, you must remember the reason you started in the first place. That's why it is essential to inspire purpose more than profit.

In a moving video talk, comedian Michael Jr. describes the power of knowing your "why," according to Naphtali Hoff, Psy.D, a contributor at the HuffPost. In it, he showed an audience a clip from a different event, in which he asked a member of that audience to sing the opening stanzas from "Amazing Grace." The gentleman, a music teacher, began in a deep baritone and sang the refrain flawlessly. After praising his performance, the comedian asked the teacher to do it again, but this time painted a scenario of sincere appreciation, such as a family member being released from prison.

Not surprisingly, the second performance far outshone the first. This time, the song was performed with added feelings and emotions. The words were more animated, and the tone was more profound and more vibrant. Michael Jr. concluded: "when you know your 'why,' then your 'what' has more impact because you're working towards your purpose." The late great Dr. Myles Munroe said the biggest tragedy in life is not death; it is life without a purpose. Your purpose keeps you alive, keeps you focused, and, most importantly, it provides the excitement and energy to keep pushing and fighting when challenges come. Gerry Anderson found this out when he first became the president of DTE Energy.

All the great leaders, all the great people I listed above, all of them faced challenges, every single one of them. They managed to push through because they understood their purpose, they consistently reminded their team about the purpose, and they realized that their purpose in life was much bigger than their own self-preservation.

You can never climb a smooth mountain and make it to the top.

Challenges are part of how we grow, how we improve, and how we become better. If you want to learn something new, if you're going to respond to changes in your environment, if you're going to remain relevant in your industry, your purpose must drive you. In Simon Sinek's now famous Ted Talk, 'How great leaders inspire action,' Sinek provided a simple but powerful model for inspirational leadership: the golden circle and the question "Why?" According to Sinek, the fundamental difference between the "Apples" of the world and everyone else is that they start with "why."

Because Apple starts with "why" when defining their company, they can attract customers who share their fundamental beliefs. As Sinek puts it, "People don't buy what you do; they buy *why* you do it." When Steve Jobs returned as the CEO of a nearly bankrupt Apple, he discontinued almost 80% of Apple's product line at the time to focus only on a few products. Jobs took the company right back to their purpose and their core and infused that purpose in the company. Apple is now one of the world's most valuable companies, disrupting industries with their breathtaking and innovative products and services, simply because the company found its why again.

In 2007, Ford was in severe trouble and closed to bankruptcy when Alan Mulally became the CEO of the company. To put Ford problem into context. The company lost 12 billion dollars in 2006, Mulally took the company back to its original mooring, which proves to be the catalyst that led to the amazing transformation of Ford. If you want to become an inspirational leader, you must always start with your purpose, start with your why it may be challenging at times, but your purpose and a shared purpose will bring you through the challenging times.

19. THE TOP 7 CHARACTERISTICS OF AN INSPIRATIONAL LEADER

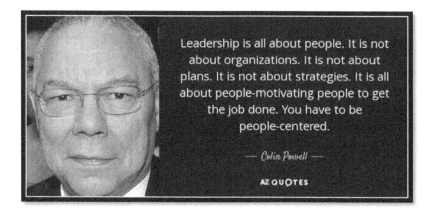

Leadership is all about people. It is not about organizations. It is not about plans. It is not about strategies. It is all about people-motivating people to get the job done. You have to be people-centered.

— Colin Powell —

AZ QUOTES

Have you ever had the privilege of working for someone who makes you feel inspired, to the point where you actually look forward to going to work? I read this story about someone who experienced an extraordinary moment at their job during a very challenging project with his team. The CEO of the company, sensing something was wrong, gave a compelling and motivational speech that left each person believing that they can achieve anything. Half an hour later, everyone left the room looking at each other and saying:

"Yes, let's do that right now, let's go for it."

The late great Dr. Myles Munroe said that great leaders could walk into a room of depressed people, and transform those people into warriors. Note the word 'Transform.' My experience has shown me that inspirational leaders are a rare breed because businesses are run by what we define as managers: people with a list of objectives to accomplish, really skilled at identifying, giving and following orders, making pressure to ensure that these are done. In many cases, businesses can be driven by managers, but what separates the great companies from the good ones, are inspirational leaders. According to Fernando Vilas, these leaders inspire others to follow them, even in very adverse situations.

Leadership is all about people, and I am 100 percent sure, your life was impacted by someone you admired dearly, during your personal or professional life. God knows I have. Inspirational leaders, for example, are a rare breed, and they often distinguish themselves from other leaders by their unique characteristics. In the book The Leadership Challenge, the authors suggested that when inspirational leadership exists, people "raise each other to higher levels of motivation and morality." These leaders instill "a sense of adventure in others, look for ways to radically alter the status quo, and ... scan the environment for new and fresh ideas."

These leaders always search for opportunities to do what has never been done. As a result, their leadership is exemplified in these five characteristics.

Inspire a shared vision

An inspirational leader's primary characteristic is to have the synergy to create visions and goals for the institution, out of the old vision. The leader must create a new vision for the institution and adequately communicate this vision to others. In The Leadership Challenge, the authors emphasize that "by using persuasive language, positive communication style, and nonverbal expressiveness, leaders breathe life into a vision shared by everyone in the organization."

Challenge the status quo

The Harvard Business Review asked more than 1,000 employees; How often have you seen senior leaders challenge the status quo. The result? 42% said never or almost never, 32% said sometimes, and 26% said fairly often or very often. Only 3% said always. Inspirational leaders, by their nature, challenge the status quo and are not afraid of change.

Enable others to act

Inspirational leaders are comfortable involving others in the decision-making process. If the leader empowers others and delegates responsibilities, followers can share in the decision-making process. They are more likely to use the participatory process to arrive at a consensus.

According to Pielstick, when leaders foster participation with others in the decision-making process, there is less likelihood of escalating the conflict to emerge. The leader has a mentality that is inclusive to all followers, including diverse and multicultural groups. They listen to everyone and seek to create an atmosphere of empowerment in their organization.

Model the way

Inspirational leaders serve as role models for their employees. Because they trust and respect the leader, they emulate this individual and internalize his or her ideals. If the leader does not demonstrate a commitment through their actions, that organization will be full of conflict and quickly become a very toxic place to work. Leaders should always walk the talk, but it becomes even more critical to do so when their organization is going through a change.

Encourage the heart

Another critical aspect of inspirational leaders is that the leader must intellectually and emotionally stimulate people. When leaders inspire and empower others, the work becomes stimulating, motivating, challenging, and fascinating. Building on their strengths and enhancing their knowledge and skills, leaders can have a transforming effect on their employees' lives by helping them stay engaged and competent in their chosen careers.

Persistence and Faith

Inspirational leaders are very persistent in the face of immense challenges. They have a real relationship, not a one night stand, but a deep commitment to faith. They never allow fear to rule their life; when they feel stuck and everything they tried is not bearing any fruit, they dig deep and bring forth their faith and never give up.

Humility

Holding any position of power can be useful for your ego, but don't let that position of power create a false sense of security. Your employees must know you're not above your shortcomings. "Leaders must not be afraid to recognize their own failures," said Joe Chiarello, owner of two Murphy Business & Financial Corporation franchises.

We all fall down at some point, but what really matters is how we pick ourselves up and learn from our mistakes. This is what helps us grow and makes us stronger." Leading by example and having transparency with your team if you do something wrong or make a bad decision can go a long way. Inspirational leaders are change agents. They exhibit characteristics that reflect a vision for the future, demonstrate an ability to influence others, provide inspiration and encouragement to others, and express high-performance expectations. The end -result of inspirational leaders is that people are motivated to succeed, and the institution is strengthened and transformed. Inspirational leaders inspire people to believe that the impossible is possible, and in the process, bring forth the best in themselves and others.

20. THE MYTH OF THE COMPLETE LEADER

Great leaders are **not** the best at everything. They find people who are **best** at **different** things and get them all on the same **team**.

~ Eileen Bistrisky

EffectiveConsulting.ca

Anewly minted CEO held a meeting with his executive team to discuss the company's growth. One of the CEO's direct reports recommended how the company can grow its market share in the next five years. The CEO, listening very attentively, was clueless about his manager's suggestion. He wondered, "should I ask a question, but if I do ask, that will reveal my lack of knowledge, and I may appear incompetent."

Most CEOs today believe that "not knowing" will somehow send a signal to their staff that the leader is somehow inept. Some people think a leader should have a complete set of skills, characteristics, and abilities to handle any problem, challenge, or opportunity that comes along. This myth of the "complete leader" can cause stress and frustration for leaders and their team, as well as damage to the organization. It's time to end this myth, and according to Deborah Ancona et al., **the sooner leaders stop trying to be all things to all people, the better off their organizations will be.**

In today's world, the executive's job is no longer to command and control but to cultivate and coordinate others' actions at all levels of the organization. Only when leaders come to see themselves as incomplete—as having both strengths and weaknesses—will they be able to make up for their missing skills by relying on others. Deborah Ancona et al. further explain that incomplete leaders differ from incompetent leaders in that they understand what they're good at and what they're not. As a result, they have sound judgment about how they can work with others to build on their strengths and offset their limitations.

No one person could possibly stay on top of everything. But the myth of the complete leader (and the attendant fear of appearing incompetent) makes many executives try to do just that, exhausting themselves and damaging their organizations in the process. The incomplete leader knows when to let go; for example before Richard Branson created his business empire, he grappled with dyslexia. Branson said this forced him to master the art of delegation, a skill that many intelligent people struggle with, and he quickly found people who were much better at things he wasn't capable of doing.

The incomplete leader builds leadership and knows that leadership exists throughout the organizational hierarchy and has a distinct advantage of tapping into expertise, vision, new ideas, and commitment when necessary.

102

By contrast, many incompetent managers and "leaders" attempt to foster trust, optimism, and consensus but often reap anger, cynicism, and conflict because they have difficulty relating to others. Anyone can bark out orders. It doesn't take strength to yell at people, write them up or blame them for mistakes. It doesn't take courage to boss people around in private and public when the organizational chart gives them the power to do that. It is the height of cowardice to manage a team with the presumption that they have to listen to you, because of your job title relative to theirs.

Managers who bluster and threaten people are weak and fake leaders who bully people all the time and don't have the muscles to manage any other way. They believe leaders should have all the answers, someone with superhero powers who should try to be everything to everyone, but these "so-called Leaders" often get burned out and lash out aggressively when things don't go as expected. Some people think a leader should have a complete set of skills, characteristics, and abilities to handle any problem, challenge, or opportunity that comes along. That's the height of incompetence. A real leader doesn't intimidate anyone.

They don't need to, and they wouldn't dream of it. Incomplete leaders create a complementary balance of people around them to help the organization achieve its vision, goals, and objectives because they are uniquely aware of their strengths and weaknesses. An incomplete leader takes the time and invests his/her energy into building a team because real leaders know that the key to successful leadership is influence, not authority, according to Ken Blanchard.

Great Leaders are not the smartness in the room

103

The most influential businesses are built on the smartest people – not on one person. According to Brian Scudamore, I've learned that strong leaders don't fight to have the first and last word. They listen to their teams, ask the right questions, and give everyone the chance to contribute. Instead of trying to do it all, find people who can do it better. With the right people in place, you can take a step back to focus on your strengths – like leading your team and planning your company's future.

Great leaders aren't know-it-alls who continuously try to outshine everyone. They admit when they're wrong and genuinely want to learn from others. It's not about being the smartest person in the room. It's about building a team with the most intelligent people you can find. You become an inspirational leader when you have the humility to build a team with people smarter than you.

In an Alison Griswold article, Alison shared an interview conducted by the New York Times with Lynn Good, CEO of Duke Energy. Lynn describes what she sees as the difference between a great leader and a smart individual. The question was one she focused on when charged with merging the staff of two companies — Progress Energy and Duke Energy — early in her tenure as chief executive.

"At a certain career level, it's no longer about whether you are the smartest subject-matter expert in the room," Good explains. "As you think about developing people through their careers, you're looking for that transition from being the smartest person in the room — and caring so much about that — to being the most effective."

As a leader, your best move is to intentionally not be the smartest person in the room. And other iconic figures would agree. As Lee Iacocca once said, "I hire people brighter than me and get out of their way." Great leaders know that their team is the backbone of the company. Any success the organization achieves comes from their employee's love of the company, the belief in the vision, and a strong attachment to the company's purpose.

21. BECOME A VISIONRY LEADER

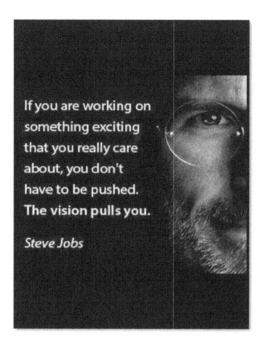

If you are working on something exciting that you really care about, you don't have to be pushed. The vision pulls you.

Steve Jobs

In 1997, Venus Williams was tennis fastest rising star. Reaching the finals of her first-ever U.S. Open as an unseeded player, and surprising the tennis world with her talent and skills. But her dad and coach, Richard Williams, said something that sounded a little crazy at the time, "Hey, my younger daughter is even better."

What! A guy said with a dazed and confused look on his face, "your daughter made it to the U.S. Open final as an unseeded player, and now you are saying your younger daughter is better." It's sounded like Tales From a Strange Land, according to David Rudder's Madman's Rant. Richard's vision was spot on; you got it right. Serena Williams is arguably the best tennis player ever? The best tennis player of all-time, male or female?

The Williams sisters have 30 grand slam singles titles each. They played each other in the finals nine times. They also have 17 doubles titles playing together in only 33 major appearances, with three gold medals in Olympic doubles. No doubt, Richard's vision of his two girls was bullseye perfect. However, I am always left dumbfounded when I read about people with the ability to see what no one else is seeing; it gives me goosebumps every time. How do they know, how did Richard know that Venus and Serena, as little girls playing on those cracked courts in Compton, with gunfire sometimes echoing in the distance, would become two of the greatest players in tennis history?

What's their secret?

Visionary leaders and great innovators follow that feeling in their heart; they know without knowing. They see what isn't yet there and create what does not yet exist. Visionaries see the way forward while the world reacts. They see something no one else can't see, and most importantly, they feel it in their heart and boldly go after it until their vision comes to fruition. According to the late great Dr. Myles Munroe, the greatest gift God ever gave us is not the gift of sight, but the gift of vision. Sight is a function of your eyes, but vision is a function of your heart. Are you a visionary leader? Here are six signs you might be.

Visionary leaders are imaginative.

Visionary people can foresee things easily. I read an article about Lee Kuan Yew of Singapore, a man who envisioned Singapore's island city to become a metropolitan first-world city.

107

From 1959 to 1990, Lee Kuan Yew remained in charge of Singapore for an uninterrupted 56 years, many years later, Singapore became precisely what Lee Kuan Yew saw it to be. One of the wealthiest and most expensive cities in the world, and it all happened in one generation! It is especially impressive since Singapore was a third world country in the 1960s.

According to Kamran Akbarzadeh, founder of Dream Achievers Academy, Vvisionaries can imagine future possibilities in their minds and then explain what they have imagined clearly. They believe things that others cannot imagine. Through their imagination, they can draw future possibilities for their organization and country.

They are big-picture oriented.

When Steve Jobs return to lead the company he co-founded in 1997, he negotiated a partnership with Microsoft that proved incredibly crucial for the company, especially the $150 million injections from Microsoft to help a failing Apple at the time. But the most critical aspect of this partnership was Jobs' ability to see the big picture. In his Macworld presentation in 1997, the excited crowd awaited the introduction of Steve Jobs to the stage. Now picture yourself at Macworld, sitting in front of the man who was like the messiah coming to save the company he co-founded, and whose vision help created an iconic company. In one 12 minute speech, Jobs dramatically changed the direction of his company forever. Jobs said:

"To make Apple healthy and prospering again, we have to let go of a few things here. We have to let go of this notion that for Apple to win, Microsoft has to lose," Jobs said. "We have to embrace the notion that for

Apple to win, Apple has to do a really good job. If others are going to help us, that's great. Because we need all the help we can get...The era of setting this up as a competition between Apple and Microsoft is over."

The ability of Jobs to see the big picture allowed Apple to become the juggernaut it is today and one of the world's most influential companies.

They share and communicate the dream/vision.

One of the big signs of visionaries is their willingness to share their vision with the world. According to Dr. Luis Calingo, Martin Luther King, Jr.shared with the world, his vision for an end to racism in America, when he delivered his "I Have a Dream" speech. By articulating a shared dream, Martin Luther King, Jr. empowered his fellow Americans to participate in a national dialogue about the achievement of his dream. Visionary leaders understand that they cannot keep the dream to themselves, because they know that they cannot get to the destination alone.

They Turn Vision Into Reality

According to Dave Lavinsky, whenever a vision is followed by action, it can be turned into reality. One crucial step of leadership is the formation of a formidable team. No single skill set is sufficient in achieving success in business. A visionary leader recognizes talent and recruits individuals with skills that contribute to the growth of the business. For example, hiring Sheryl Sandberg was one of the smartest business decisions Facebook CEO, Mark Zuckerberg, ever made.

According to Richard Feloni, Sandberg joined in March 2008 when Facebook was ready to scale and needed the insight she developed in her role as the head of Google's advertising arm, as well as her role as the chief of staff to Treasury Secretary, Larry Summers. Facebook would end 2008 with 450 employees, $272 million in revenue, at a loss of $56 million; in 2016, Facebook had more than 17,000 employees and brought in $27.6 billion in revenue, with $10.2 billion in net income. Zuckerberg had the vision to hire his weakness, which allowed Facebook to experience explosive growth to become the world's largest social media company.

They are never afraid of failures.

As mentioned earlier, true visionaries see what others cannot see, and they know there will be challenges along the way. They know they might have temporary setbacks. But they also know the great value of fulfilling their vision. Therefore, true visionaries never give up. They are not afraid of failures because they know that failures are part of the process.

JK Rowling said that failure gets such a bad rap in our society. We see thousands of best-selling books about succeeding in life, but none about how to fail. Now you're probably thinking, "Why on earth would I ever want to fail, or even worse, learn how to fail?" The truth is, failure is an essential part of life. We have just completely lost sight of its purpose.

They are positive energizers.

Another sign of true visionaries is their positive attitude, according to Kamran Akbarzadeh, founder of Dream Achievers Academy. Since visionaries are passionate about and connected with their vision, their positive energy level is typically high. They recharge people with positive energy because of their positive attitude. True visionaries are surrounded by positive people who are willing to help them achieve a shared vision.

110

Visionary leaders balance vision with action

They are not afraid of public opinion; they work to develop others and are not scared to go the extra mile to achieve their vision.

Richard Williams can lay claim to a remarkable and unprecedented legacy. But remember his backstory. According to Allen St. John, as a former sharecropper, Richard Williams saw a tennis match on TV and was shocked at the size of the check being handed to the winner. So, as a middle-aged black man, he decided to teach himself this remarkably complex game. He then wrote a 78-page plan, scrounged a shopping cart full of balls, and showed his two youngest daughters the game. He came from the most unlikely and challenging circumstances to coached his two daughters, who not only dominated but reinvented the game of tennis.

22 THE 11 MAJOR ATTRIBUTES OF LEADERSHIP

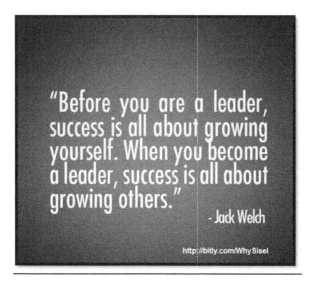

Have you ever had the great privilege and good fortune to work with, and for a leader who inspires you by their words, and most importantly, by their actions? If you did, you are among the fortunate few, because far too many people in leadership roles are ill-equipped to lead with effectiveness. As a result, many people are only going to work to make a living instead of making a difference.

In 1937, Napoleon Hill wrote his book, Think and Grow Rich after studying the traits and habits of 500 self-made millionaires of his time. In the book, Hill introduces the world to the 11 attributes of major leadership, but what is quite amazing, and to be quite honest, I am still in awe with this book; is how relevant these attributes were in 2018.

If you have not read the book, I implore you to read it, especially if you are responsible for leading people. Here are the 11 attributes of effective leadership, as outlined by Napoleon Hill.

Willingness to Assume Full Responsibility.

The successful leader must be willing to assume responsibility for the mistakes and the shortcomings of his/her followers. If they try to shift the responsibility, he/she will not remain the leader. If one of their followers makes a mistake and shows themself to be incompetent, the leader must consider that he/she failed.

Definiteness of Decision.

The person who wavers in their decisions shows that they are not sure of themself and, as a result, cannot lead others successfully.

Definiteness of Plans.

A successful leader must plan his/her work and work their plan. A leader who moves by guesswork, without practical, definite plans, is comparable to a ship without a rudder. Sooner or later, they will land on the rocks.

Unwavering Courage

Based upon knowledge of self and of one's occupation. No follower wishes to be led by a leader who lacks self-confidence and courage.

A Keen Sense of Justice.

Without a sense of fairness and justice, no leader can command and retain the respect of their followers.

Self Control.

The person who cannot control themselves can never control others. Self-control sets a mighty example for one's followers.

The Habit of Doing More Than Paid For.

One of the penalties of leadership is the necessity of willingness upon the part of the leader to do more than requires.

A Pleasing Personality.

No slovenly, careless, or unpleasant person can become a successful leader. Leadership calls for respect.

Sympathy and Understanding.

The successful leader must be in sympathy with their followers. A leader must understand their team issues as well as their problems as well.

Mastery of Detail.

Successful leadership calls for mastery of details of the leader's position. According to Matt Ladin, 75 years ago, Hill wrote: "The relation of employer and employee, or of leader and follower, in the future, will be one of mutual cooperation, based upon an equitable division of the profits of a business. In the future, the relationship between employer and employee will be more like a partnership; then it has been in the past."

Someone who can follow a leader most efficiently is usually the person who develops into leadership most rapidly. An intelligent follower has many advantages, including the OPPORTUNITY TO ACQUIRE KNOWLEDGE FROM HIS/HER LEADER. Wishful thinking, perhaps?

According to Matt, collectively, it would appear that we still have a lot of work to do.

23 WHERE DID YOU GET YOUR LEADERSHIP PHILOSOPHY FROM?

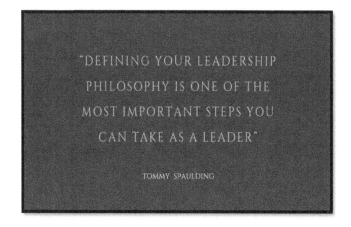

"DEFINING YOUR LEADERSHIP PHILOSOPHY IS ONE OF THE MOST IMPORTANT STEPS YOU CAN TAKE AS A LEADER"

TOMMY SPAULDING

I n 1919 when Belgium colonized Rwanda, they immediately divided the people based on their appearance. The Belgians came in and restructured all of Rwanda to reflect their customs, and how they wanted to rule. Before they invaded Rwanda, there was no distinction between the Tutsi and Hutus; they were one ethnic group.

The only difference between the two was that the Hutus were mostly agriculturalists, and Tutsi were cattle breeders. The Belgians separated the people of Rwanda into these two races, even when they did not know the original tribes of the people. The Tutsis were considered the superior race because of their European-like features. I can remember watching Hotel Rwanda, and I was utterly horrified by the number of people killed in the massacre during the 100 days from the 7th of April to mid-July 1994. The Rwandan genocide, also known as the genocide against the Tutsi and moderate Hutus, was a mass slaughter. Members of the Hutu majority government directed it with an estimated 500,000 to 1,000,000 Rwandans killed; 70% of the Tutsi population.

I read Immaculee Ilibagiza's book Left to Tell. I understood the reasons that caused the genocide and the generational brainwashing of people who don't know, and in many instances, have no appreciation for how historical events shape the world's philosophy on leadership and life.

The Origin of Leadership

The source of our modern-day leadership is attributed to the Romans, who adopted their leadership philosophies from the Greeks. Great thinkers of the Greeks, like Plato, Socrates, and Aristotle, created the world's leadership theory that influences the way we lead today in our modern 21st-century organization and societies.

These famous Greeks philosophers invented things like democrata, known as democracy. They were the first to develop the concept of citizenship, invented words like polites, known as politics, and the first to study human control and manipulation techniques, for instance. These great "thinkers," believed that if you were born with unique traits, you were automatically a leader. For example, they believed leadership is a result of inherent birth traits in the individual's personality and nature. The majority who do not possess these traits are destined to be led. For example, if you were born with a sharply pointed nose, blue eyes, fair skin, and thin lips, you were born a leader. The Greeks also believed that certain people were chosen by the Gods and appointed to the elite position of leadership over the unfortunate people. The Greeks believed leadership is reserved for the few selected by a divine power to control, manage, and direct the life, future, fortunes, and aspirations of the unchosen.

They believed that leadership is the product of a forceful personality. This theory emerges from the belief that leadership is the result of an authoritarian, no-nonsense, hard-driving, impatient, quick-tempered, and moody personality. This false perception comes from the idea that people are fundamentally incompetent and naturally lazy. They have got to be pushed to get things done. However, the evidence has always defied this belief, showing that people are most productive and cooperative when they are inspired rather than forced.

So, when the Roman Empire collapsed and Europe was formed and by the way, many European countries, as we know it today, were all part of the Roman Empire; the European countries naturally continued these misguided philosophies of leadership because of their beliefs. Colonization and killing of the people who were living in these countries were natural because they were not born with the traits, so they were not chosen by the Gods, and as a result, they were born a slave. If you ever wonder why slaves were treated as non-humans, you got your answer and why the world sat back and did absolutely nothing to stop the slaughter of innocent women and children in Rwanda.

So the question I want to ask you is this: Where did you get your leadership philosophy from?
What or who influences the way you lead? Do you or did you follow these leadership philosophies; no wonder 80% of our workforce today is not

engaged. You know the Greeks were the ones who also introduced the word charisma which means, "favor freely given" or "gift of grace."

The Greeks believed that certain individuals who possessed a unique measure of charisma were destined to lead. For example, they believed people who are extroverts are natural leaders. This theory has been accepted by many, even in our world today, and it has frustrated the life of many as well. Some people wholeheartedly believe this nonsense, when some of our greatest leaders were and are very introverted people.

Some people believe leadership is about power, dominance, rule, ask no questions, give no explanation; they believe they were born to rule, and people should bow down and worship them. I have seen CEO's and people who called themselves leaders walk into a room for example, and the room was automatically filled with fear; I tell you, the room became so stiff, like a starch shirt fresh from the dry cleaners, you could take a knife and cut the tension in half.

Some people feed off that kind of leadership for their own self-importance; fear and intimidation are the order of the day, and they rule with an iron fist with people afraid to even ask a question or make a suggestion.

"the way you think about people determines how you lead them or destroy them" Dr. Myles Munroe.

What kind of leadership is that? How do you expect to get the best out of your people if the environment is so intimidating? That's not leadership; that's a dictatorship. No one and I repeat no one, should ever settle for that kind of situation and don't let anyone fool you to believe, no other options exist when the world is overflowing with opportunities. All you need is to get your thinking straight.

It is so difficult to change some peoples' philosophies on leadership because of their belief that was passed down from generation to generation. Leadership is about people and self-discovery; you were born to have dominion over your gifts, not people. Become a slave for your gift and serve that gift to the world. Inspiration is the highest form of leadership, and you become a leader when you are of service to the world, not by the number of people serving you.

Be very wary of people who called themselves leaders; the colonizers tried and, in many instances, succeeded in their quest to divide the people based on their own twisted leadership thinking and perverted agendas. It's up to us now to change these practices and mind-set because leadership is all about people, inspiring people to believe in the impossible, and inspiring people to have dominance over their gifts, never over people.

24. WHEN YOU GET THE ENVIRONMENT RIGHT GREAT THINGS HAPPEN

> When a flower doesn't bloom,
> you fix the environment in which
> it grows, not the flower.
>
> Alexander Den Heijer

D avid Marquet became the Captain of the Santa Fe, the worst performing submarine in the Navy's history. Marquet knew very little about this sub because he was initially selected to captain the USS Olympia, a nuclear-powered attack submarine, he studied for over a year.

During a simple drill to simulate a fault with the sub reactor, Captain Marquet ordered, "ahead two-thirds." The officer on deck repeated the order, "ahead two-thirds."

Nothing happened.

Captain Marquet noticed the helmsman looking very unsettled. Marquet asked, "what's the problem," the helmsman pointed out that there were no two-thirds in the electric propulsion mode, unlike all his previous submarines. The officer was asked, "did you know there were no two-thirds" the officer responded "yes" but repeated the command knowing it was wrong.

Now Captain Marquet did not have the luxury of changing his crew, unlike what typically takes place in most business organizations. Captain Marquet realized that the leader-follower environment his team has grown accustomed too failed, and if he had any chance to turn around the performance of this sub, the environment must change. Marquet began treating his crew as leaders; giving control, not taking control; he changed the environment. Not long after, the Santa Fe went from the worst performing submarine in the Navy to the best navel sub in the history of the Navy.

As leaders, when you get the environment right, great things can happen because it's never the people; it's the environment; and as the leader, you have the responsibility to ensure you create a place your people love to come to. We spend so much of our time at work, so it's only natural to feel some sense of comfort while at work. Fear Has No Place At Work and no amount of yelling, shouting, or screaming can transform any environment into one that allows their people to be their very best. It's quite amazing that many people in management positions will resonate with creating an environment of fear to get their people to work.

All the research in the world has proven that fear base environments are not sustainable and are incredibly damaging to the morale and sanity of anyone who has to work in that kind of environment. Fear has no place in work, it may have some impact in the short term, but it is never sustainable in the long run. Many leaders fall victim to blaming their staff without looking in the mirror; we are not meeting our projection; it must be the staff; we are underperforming, we need a new team. As a result, all kinds of changes occur without really looking at the root cause of the problem.

People Don't Leave Companies, They Leave Lousy Management, and Great leaders set up shields, according to Lori Goler, Janelle Gale, Brynn Harrington, and Adam Grant, to protect their employees from toxicity. Passion is contagious, and the more negative energy that drips into the organization's culture, the more dysfunctional the organization will become. The 'quietness' of typically motivated employees is an organizational alarm that leadership needs to recognize as a sign that the culture is becoming or has become toxic. This is an excellent indicator that something is amidst, and as a result, the leadership needs to act on it, according to Jonathan Mills.

The Simple Things Make A Huge Difference and appreciation is one of life's greatest motivators, so when we take the time to let people know that we value them, it inspires them to continue doing even more. That's precisely why gratitude is the ultimate gift that keeps on giving, according to Amy Rees Anderson. There is no doubt that when we say the words "thank you," for example, we make the other person feel important and valued, which helps create a great work environment and improve the self-image of their people.

When the fundamentals of a company are in place (purpose, vision, and values) and everyone is singing from the same hymnbook with the leader leading by example, your organization will find its pulse of existence to become one of the best in the world. David Marquet transformed his underperforming sub into a world-class entity because he understood that it's never the people; it's the environment.

25. LEADERS WHO CREATE FEAR-BASED ORGANISATIONS ARE DOOMED TO FAIL, HERE'S WHY

I am not impressed by your position, title and money. I am impressed by how you treat others.

D avid just escaped from a full-time job in a toxic work environment where the best employees quit, and the worst people got promoted to management jobs. The people with all the ideas were shunned and pushed aside; they soon left the organization while the tush-kissers with no plans got promoted.

The harder David worked, the worse he got treated. When a completely unqualified person got promoted to be his manager because that manager had a personal relationship with one of the VPs, that was the last straw; David resigns. It was hard for him to leave the company, he worked so hard for, but the minute he was out of there, he felt a huge weight lifted off his shoulders.

I read this story from Liz Ryan's article in Forbes, and it is so reminiscent of so many people experiences in many organizations all over the world. Great employees, who came into the organization with an inspired heart and a spark in their eyes ready to make a difference, got uninspired and demotivated when they soon realized this is not the right environment for anyone to work. It's quite amazing that many people in management and leadership positions will resonate with creating an environment of fear to get their people to work. I don't understand it; all the research in the world has proven that fear-based leadership or management does not work; it may in the short term, but the quality of work will be average at best and never sustainable in the long run.

According to Liz Ryan, what is a fearful manager's greatest fear? It's not that the business might fail; no, their greatest fear is that somebody working near them might challenge them. A fearful manager's ego is stronger than the fear of business failure. According to Jim Harter, Gallup's Chief Scientist, it is the rite of passage in most organizations to promote someone based on their performance on the job. So if you are very good at sales, or accounting, or any number of specialties—and stay around a long time, the next step in your progression is to be promoted to manager.

But the talents that make a person successful in a previous, non-management role are rarely the same ones that will make them excel as a manager or as a leader. Research shows that new managers are usually promoted without the skills needed to be good managers or leaders, and 47% of companies do not have a new supervisor training program to help them bridge the gap, according to Ken Blanchard.

Sadly, when companies promote people into a management position and do not provide the necessary training, they end up with a host of bosses and few leaders. According to Liz, lousy employees get promoted to lofty positions in fear-based organizations because they are non-threatening to the leaders. Non-threatening is the best thing you can be in a toxic environment. It's the principal job requirement.

You have to be very careful about the people who call themselves leaders, especially those with Pseudo - Leadership tendencies. Many of these people are only concerned about their well-being, nothing else. Fearful employees stick around because they got so institutionalized they believe every company has the same management or culture. For these employees, it's typical for a manager and their employees to engage in gossip, typical for their manager to shout at their staff, usual to work in a constant state of fear, and to routinely hide from their manager if something goes wrong.

Yes, hide, you will not believe the kind of environment some people have to endure. It's hard for some of these employees to see their fear when they are in the middle of it, according to Liz. Still, when you're out of that toxic environment, you soon realize how toxic it was and how much the organization's management contributed to the creation of that environment.

Fear has no place in management and leadership, absolutely none; if anyone uses fear as a strategy to get their people to work, that person has no place managing and leading anyone; None! Fear dis-empowers and turns employees' attention inward instead of outward, according to Tom Flick. Staff members who are driven by fear go into survival mode. They are no longer interested in the company's outcome, the quality of the product or service, or the customer experience. Instead, they're concerned with keeping their jobs and not stepping on toes.

The effects of fear-based tactics can negatively impact employee engagement, customer experience, and even brand reputation, according to Rose Krivich. When employees are stressed and fearful, this dissatisfaction can seep into conversations with clients. Their frustrations with their' organization's culture may be voiced word of mouth or via the internet, serving as a red flag to potential candidates. Never settle for a toxic, fear-based organization; it's not good for your professional development, health, and energy; there are many options out there, take advantage of all because you deserve better.

CONCLUSION

"If you think leadership is about you, oh boy, your ego has led you astray. Leadership has little to do with you and everything to do with those you lead. If you think leadership is about the bottom line, think again; it's about the people. Without the people, there is no bottom line."

Mike Myatt CEO of N2growth.

To lead in this generation requires change, especially the "old school" managers who believe that employees should come to work every day for 20 years, do the same mundane task repeatedly without complaint, retire, get their pension, go home, and live happily ever after.

Consider your leadership and management style; is it adaptable to this generation. Are you inspiring this generation to be the best they can be, are you willing to admit that times have changed and as such, your leadership style should also change. This generation is not going anyway, and to get the best from this group of employees, your leadership approach should reflect the changes in our environment.

Think about it for a moment. As a leader, you have an incredible opportunity to change someone's life every single day. Because your leadership role is so important, you owe it to yourself and your team to continually develop your skills as an inspirational leader or to become one. When you are the leader, you are often held to high expectations, you are consistently under scrutiny, and you set the tone for the entire company to follow.

According to Simon Sinek, leadership is not about being in charge; it's all about taking care of those in your charge. Inspirational leadership should exist at every level of an organization to positively influence your team's success. Everyone was born with a gift and have the potential to be great at something.

Great leaders have that skill to facilitate, encourage, and empower that greatness in their team. But your self-development is paramount to your team's success, and this means being wise enough to recognize your weak points, and humble enough to work on correcting them. We need inspirational leaders; we need to inspire this generation and the next generation and the next generation on what great leadership is all about. According to Drucker, we need leaders who can lift a person's vision to higher sights, raise a person's performance to a higher standard, and build a personality beyond its normal limitations.

Real leadership is all about people and inspiring people to believe that the impossible is possible. When leaders can inspire a group of people to perform beyond their standard limitations, great things will happen. As a result, we can now make a difference in the lives of our team, our community, our country, and by extension, the world.

ABOUT THE AUTHOR

Gifford Thomas is the founder of Leadership First and one of the leading voices on inspirational leadership. Gifford has coached and mentored leaders from all over the world to believe in themselves, believe in their gifts and to use their influence to make a difference in their company, their team, their community and by extension the world each and every day.

Gifford Holds an MBA from Henley Business School, University of Reading and a B.A. (HONS) Business Management Degree from Anglia Ruskin University. Gifford is a member of Harvard Business Review Advisory Council, a Council member with GLG, an advisor with visaQ Inc out of Japan, and one of the leading writers on Quora for Leadership Development.

DISCOVER OTHER TITLES BY GIFFORD THOMAS

ORDER YOUR COPY TODAY

★ ★ ★ ★ ★

""Gifford really does communicate the importance of communication for change management in this well-structured and articulate book. The subject matter is conveyed in a very engaging manner with a good balance of theory, case study examples, opinion and practical advice. Those of you familiar with change management frameworks will find this book enhances your understanding; those new to the area will find the book a useful guide."

Mike Green
Director ~ Transitional Space
Visiting Executive Fellow ~
Henley Business School, University of
Reading

CONNECT WITH ME

Believe In The Impossible
600,000+ Followers

At Leadership First, we are inspiring our 600,000+ leaders every day to believe that the impossible is possible and helping our leaders create an environment where their people are inspired and motivated at work. We are inspiring leaders to create an environment free from toxic, fearful and intimating management practices by publishing the very best inspirational leadership quotes and articles from the best leadership minds in the world. We are dedicated to helping every leader create an excellent organization and to provide a daily cup of inspiration for all leaders.

You can follow us on LinkedIn, Facebook and Instagram for all your daily inspiration.

Made in the USA
Las Vegas, NV
21 October 2021